DEER & DEER HUNTING'S

GUIDE TO
BETTER
BOW-
HUNTING

Published by

Krause Publications a division of F+W, A Content + eCommerce Company
700 East State Street • Iola, WI 54990-0001
715-445-2214 • 888-457-2873
www.krausebooks.com

To order books or other products call toll-free 1-800-258-0929
or visit us online at www.shopdeerhunting.com

ISBN-13: 978-1-4402-3082-0
ISBN-10: 1-4402-3082-X

Designed by Al West
Edited by Brian Lovett

Printed in USA

contents

introduction

YOU CAN BECOME A BETTER BOWHUNTER

▶ BOWHUNTING FOR WHITE-TAILED DEER has witnessed an explosion of interest in the past 20 years. As whitetail populations have soared and bowhunting gear and tactics have gone mainstream, more and more deer hunters are picking up stick and string to chase their favorite quarry.

Today, the sport ranks higher in participation than almost any other form of hunting after whitetail gun hunting. In fact, archery has become so popular the National Archery in the Schools Program is set to surpass Little League Baseball in participation. This surge in interest means bowhunting is still relatively new for many folks. In fact, beginners and intermediate archers make up a large portion of America's 3.2 million bowhunters — and these folks are hungry for expert information. Even seasoned archery veterans find the sport is continually evolving with new, cutting-edge products entering the market every year. Add it all up and the hunting world is hungry for practical and comprehensive archery insights.

Along the way *Deer & Deer Hunting* magazine has been recognized as a leader in sharing the techniques and gear that make us better archers and hunters. This book is a compilation of the very best tips and strategies from our No. 1 archery expert, Bob Robb.

Inside these pages, Robb shares shooting advice, insights on critical gear, bowhunting techniques and tons of helpful hints for in-the-field archery success.

Presented in a straightforward, no-nonsense approach, *Deer & Deer Hunting's Guide to Better Bowhunting* highlights all the little things archers can do to get more out of their archery gear. It offers real-world examples and examines the latest products that can help you in the woods. In fact, the detailed advice will help any archer — from the Rocky Mountains to the target range. If you've ever wondered about which broadheads to use, why we miss angled shots or what type of bow is best for your shooting style, this book will answer those questions ... and more!

This cutting-edge information is sure to make you a better bowhunter and shooter, whether you are a beginner or seasoned expert.

Welcome to the world better bowhunting. You can become a better bowhunter. ■

chapter 1

12 STEPS TO BETTER BOWHUNTING

▶ WITH SERIOUS WHITETAIL SEASON UPON US, the last thing you want to do is rush off to your favorite stand and find out that some little thing you never anticipated turns that "gimme" shot into a "goner."

That's why final preparations are so important.

The key is to anticipate problems before they happen and solve them at home. To that end, here are some things you may not think about much ... until it is too late.

1. FINE-TUNE YOUR ARROWS. Before hunting season, make sure you have a dozen broadhead-arrow shaft combinations that fly like laser beams. Shoot every one of them at least a couple of times to ensure they are flying right and also impact where the sight pins say they should. Weigh the fletched shaft and broadhead, both separately and together, the goal being to have a quiver full of finished shafts that weigh within 3 to 5 grains of each other. When it's time to hunt, either re-sharpen your blades or replace them with scalpel-sharp blades from a new pack.

2. SIGHT IN WITH BROADHEADS. Beginning in late summer, I quit shooting field tips altogether. If you have been using field tips and are just now switching to broadheads, make sure you practice with

Even new bows with "no-stretch" bowstrings will have the strings stretch at first, which can rotate the peep into a different position after a while.

exactly the same arrow/broadhead combination you will hunt with. This means first shooting them through paper to make sure the bow is precisely tuned with this combination. You'll probably have to make some arrow-rest adjustments to achieve this. Then re-sight the bow using the broadheads. Do not be satisfied with a bow that is only "sort of" tuned!

3. CHECK YOUR BOWSTRING. Check the string and cable system for wear, paying attention to those areas where it rolls through the wheels and, if you do not use a string loop, where your release attaches directly to the string. Then lightly wax it.

4. PEEP CLOSELY. Do you use a peep sight without a rubber tube that forces it back into the proper position every time? Then make sure yours does turn back the right way. Even new bows with those supposed "no-stretch" bowstrings will have the strings minutely stretch at first, which, of course, rotates the peep into a different position after a while, so check it, fix it and then use an indelible marker above and below the peep to mark its exact position.

5. LOCK IT DOWN. Check all the screws that secure accessories to the bow, including your quiver and sight, and make sure they are locked down.

6. LUBRICATE IT. It's time to lubricate the bow's axles and also the moving parts of your release aid. I do so with a graphite product that will not freeze when the weather turns bitter.

7. PAD IT. I pad the heck out of everything that has even the smallest chance of making noise on stand with stick-on moleskin or fleece. The bottom of my bow sight, the arrow shelf, arrow rest prongs — they all get covered up. I also have covered my entire laser rangefinder in moleskin, then covered that with a layer of the same tape hockey players wrap their sticks with. Hockey tape is an awesome product for bowhunters because it is tough, quiet and, best of all, does not get stiff when temperatures drop below freezing.

> THE LAST THING YOU WANT TO DO IS RUSH OFF TO YOUR FAVORITE STAND AND FIND OUT THAT SOME LITTLE THING YOU NEVER ANTICIPATED TURNS THAT "GIMME" SHOT INTO A "GONER."

8. TRY SPECIFICITY TRAINING. This is a term coined by exercise physiologists when training athletes to perform to their maximum potential at specific tasks. For example, a sprinter trains his legs and cardiovascular system so he can run his fastest, and doesn't spend a lot of time lifting heavy weights with his upper body. For bowhunters, that means replicating in practice as closely as possible those shots you will most likely get at deer. That means that, while standing at a target line on the range is great practice, shooting from an elevated platform is much better as a final tune-up for tree-stand hunting. If you hunt from a ground blind, practice shooting from the sitting position. As it gets closer to hunting, I like to wear my hunting clothes, put my binoculars and laser rangefinder around my neck just as I would when hunting, then play games with myself as I go through my mental shot checklist.

9. PACK SMART. Organize your daypack to the point where you know exactly where everything is located, from snacks and drinks to deer calls to spare clothing and equipment. That way, you won't be missing a vital piece of gear before heading afield.

10. STAND AND DELIVER. If the last time you looked at your tree stands was when you pulled them last season, the time to check them out before this season is right now. Make sure all the bolts, screws and straps are in good working order, and lubricate any joints or moving parts that might squeak.

11. POWER UP. Is there anything worse than heading to the woods and have a flashlight battery burn out? Or have the range-finder not fire at the wrong time because the battery is too weak? Spend 10 bucks now and replace all of your batteries.

12. DE-FOG OPTICS. To help keep water and fog from wrecking my vision in bad weather, I simply use the same RainX I use on my car windshield on optics lenses. It works great. ∎

chapter 2

WHY YOU NEED A 40-YARD PIN

▶ BOWHUNTING WHITETAILS IS A GAME conducive to thick cover, tight quarters and close shots. That most bowhunters set their stands for in-your-face encounters is highlighted by a survey I saw recently. This study asked archery pro shop owners — guys and gals who speak with thousands of customers annually about their deer hunting — what these folks had to say about their shots at deer. The survey showed that the average bow shot at a whitetail deer is somewhere between 21 and 25 yards.

Be that as it may, my standard whitetail bow has sight pins set for 20, 30, 40 and 50 yards, all distances at which I practice regularly with broadheads. I submit that if you would do the same, your chances of taking more and bigger deer would increase.

A shining example occurred on Nov. 11, 1999, in Brown County, Ill., when I killed the biggest buck of my life with any weapon, a perfect 10 netting 180⅝ inches. I released the arrow when he was 42 yards out, because there would not have been a chance for a closer shot. The buck entered a small greenfield at 4 p.m., scent-checking field scrapes for sign of a hot doe, and was making the rounds across the field from my tree. I had to take the shot sitting down, or my cameraman and I would have been busted. Had I not had a 40-yard pin and practiced until shooting at that distance was as comfortable as a pair of well-worn shoes, I would have watched that deer walk out of my life.

That's not the only buck I've taken at what most bowhunters consider "long range." Fortunately, I have enough time to practice enough to make these shots feel routine. As someone who spends a lot of time bowhunting the West for mule deer, elk and bears, I've learned that the farther out I can make an accurate shot with broadheads, the better my chances are at punching a tag and not having to eat "tag soup" at season's end. There are several reasons you should consider learning to shoot at longer range, too.

LONG-DISTANCE PRACTICE WILL MAKE YOU A MUCH BETTER BOW SHOT, REGARDLESS OF WHETHER OR NOT YOU EVER TAKE A LONG-RANGE SHOT AT GAME.

First and foremost, please understand I am not advocating taking poor shots at game. Each individual has his or her own personal maximum effective shooting range (MESR). If you are not comfortable and confident taking shots out past 20 or 25 yards, then by all means don't. Ever. However, extending your own MESR will give you several advantages. By practicing at longer ranges, you'll find that those typical 15- to 25-yard shots seem like slam dunks.

There's nothing like broadhead practice at 40 or 50 yards to make you focus intently on everything about your shooting, including your shooting form, the mechanics of your release, and your equipment. Minor flaws in your shooting form, often indiscernible at 20 yards, are magnified at 40. A bow-and-arrow set-up that is not perfectly in tune and generating dart-like arrow flight is incapable of producing tight arrow groups at 40 yards. Long-distance practice will make you

a much better bow shot, regardless of whether or not you ever take a long-range shot at game.

To be able to shoot at long distance requires a perfectly tuned bow-and-arrow set-up. It's all about being able to place your arrows in the bull's-eye shot after shot

The building blocks of accurate bow shooting begin with a well-tuned bow-and-arrow set-up that fits you perfectly, has a draw weight that is not too heavy for you to handle and has a let-off you are comfortable with.

"Probably the most important issue in choosing a new bow is to not get one with too heavy a draw weight," said Jim Velasquez, public relations coordinator for BowTech. "With today's technology, you get more energy from less poundage than we did just a few years ago, and thus the average archer can enjoy pulling a lighter draw-weight bow with the same performance of an older, heavier-weight bow."

Once you have the right bow, it's been tuned and your arrows are flying like laser beams, start challenging yourself. If you are comfortable at making 20- to 30-yard shots, step back and try some 35-yarders. At first you'll find it tough to keep your arrows consistently in or near the bull. Stick with it long enough and before you know it, you'll think 35-yard shots are a "gimme." Now it's time to move back and try a couple of 40-yard shots. The next thing you know you'll have a 50-yard pin, and be smacking the bull's-eye more often than not.

A long shot at a deer should not be taken without due consideration to many factors, all of which must be processed by your internal computer on a case-by-case basis. If conditions are wrong — high winds, poor visibility, extreme cold, skittish deer, etc. — I absolutely won't take a long shot. I also never attempt a long shot unless I have been able to use my laser rangefinder and know exactly how far it is.

However, when everything is just right, you can bet your britches I'll take those shots with confidence. Even out to 40 yards. There's no reason it cannot be the same for you, too. ■

chapter 3

LONG SHOTS vs. TAKING FLYERS

▶ WITH THE POSSIBLE EXCEPTION of religion, politics or the merits of different brands of whiskey, few things can heat a bowhunting camp debate faster than the subject of the farthest distances at which a skilled archer should actually take a shot at a white-tailed deer.

Each bowhunter has a different shooting ability. No one else shoots exactly the same way, or with the exact same degree of skill. Additionally, no two bowhunters perceive a target identically, even under identical conditions. Shooting is an individual thing. However, one of the most important points in all of bow hunting is for each individual to recognize his own shooting abilities and limitations — and stay within them at all times.

We all must learn and remember that each shot presents a unique set of problems that must be overcome — distance is only one of them. Other factors can include poor light, strong winds, too much brush, too many deer or the animal standing at the wrong angle.

Experience is the most important piece of equipment a bow hunter can take into the field. All the new high-tech doo-dads are terrific, but they can never take the place of your own ability to size up each situation, make judgments based on past experiences and decide

whether or not the time is right to take the shot.

Experience is time spent in the woods — during and out of hunting

Unless you can put 90 percent of your broadheads into the vitals, you should not take a shot at a deer at that distance.

season. It's also being around the game you're hunting, acquiring an intangible feel for the animal and an ability to anticipate its actions. It's time spent honing your hunting skills. It's familiarity with chosen bow-and-arrow setup, how it draws, how long you can hold it at full draw, just how it settles in your hand, the trajectory of your arrows. It's how well you can judge distance to the target. And it's how well you shoot your bow with broadhead-tipped arrows.

First and foremost, you should strive to extend what I call your MESR — or maximum effective shooting range — as much as you can. Most tree-stand hunters I know, have difficulty making a shot beyond 40 yards. Yet, with today's incredible compound bows, carbon arrows, low-profile broadheads, precision sights and a laser rangefinder, 40-yard shots are truthfully within the capability of most of us.

However, to become this kind of shooter requires dedication and attention to detail. It all begins with a bow-and-arrow setup that fits you perfectly, you are comfortable shooting, and that has been paper-tuned with the exact same arrows and broadheads you'll be hunting with.

Forget field point shooting. If you want to know exactly how your hunting arrows fly at distance, you'll destroy at least one broadhead target each year during practice sessions. Also, the importance of meticulously tuning your setup cannot be overemphasized. If your arrows have any wobble at all, they will not hit precisely where you want them to at long distance.

Extending your MESR is a simple process. Start shooting at the distance you are most comfortable with. That might be 20 yards. After laying your arrows in the bull's-eye, back up 5 yards. Keep practicing until you can place 90 percent of your hunting arrows in the X-ring. Then, move back another 5 yards, and repeat. Keep the process going until you get to the point where you are not getting them into the bull's-eye. It might be 30 yards, it might be 50 yards, but you'll know what it is. Unless you can put 90 percent of your broadheads into the vitals, you should not take a shot at a deer at that distance.

KNOWING THE EXACT DISTANCE TO THE TARGET IS EVERYTHING. TESTS CONDUCTED BY THE MILITARY HAVE SHOWN THAT THE AVERAGE PERSON CANNOT ACCURATELY JUDGE DISTANCE PAST 35 OR 40 YARDS.

Of course, this does not occur in one range session. Fatigue and the ability to keep concentrating are limiting factors. It is much better to shoot fewer arrows with proper shooting form and good concentration than a lot of arrows when you are tired and not paying attention. What you'll discover is that you really have to concentrate on proper shooting mechanics to consistently make the shot at longer distances. You'll also find that after shooting well at 50 yards, 30-yard shots are easy as pie.

Knowing the exact distance to the target is everything. Tests conducted by the military have shown that the average person cannot accurately judge distance past 35 or 40 yards. Yet, without a precise knowledge of how far away the target is, you're going to miss the shot. That's why using a laser rangefinder is so important.

How far is too far? Only you can answer that question for yourself. I do know this: The two largest bucks I have ever killed were arrowed at 42 and 46 yards, and those shots were the only ones they were going to give me.

Clint Eastwood, playing Dirty Harry Callahan, put it simply: "A man's got to know his limitations."

I do. And while I still work hard to get shots at deer at 20 or 25 yards, I want to be able to make the longer shot if I have to. ■

chapter 4

5 REASONS WE MISS SLAM-DUNKS

▶ ANY WHITETAIL BOWHUNTER who tells you he has never missed a shot is either lying or has not been hunting all that long. All of us have blown a slam dunk shot at some point in our lives. After wiping the egg off our faces, we then ask ourselves how it could have happened.

Here are the five top reasons most archers pooch that easy shot, and how to avoid these mistakes this fall.

1. LACK OF PRACTICE

How many of your buddies grab their archery equipment the weekend before they plan to go hunting, give it a quick once-over, and head out? We don't all fall in this category, but some archers do. Many of them miss easy shots.

A serious deer hunter knows how critical it is to shoot arrows prior to hunting season. This is important for so many reasons, including making sure the bow is tuned and shooting broadheads perfectly, that your sights are dead-on, and that your muscles are back in shape after a long summer.

It is also imperative to practice shooting the same way you'll be hunting. That means from an elevated platform if you hunt from a tree stand, or from a stool if you hunt from a ground blind. It means putting on big, bulky hunting clothes — including your tree stand safety harness — and practicing reaching up and getting your bow off the hook, attaching your release, drawing, picking a spot, aiming and making the shot.

2. EQUIPMENT MALFUNCTION

Here comes a deer. You get ready to shoot. Then something goes awry. Maybe the tube that straightens your peep sight pops off. Perhaps the arrow nock gets turned, causing a fletch to nick the rest. Or maybe the peep slides up the bowstring just a smidge when you draw, making the arrow impact a little low. It could be that the arrow makes a horrible screeching noise as it is drawn across the rest. Whatever happens, in bowhunting it's the little things that allow deer to keep their scalps.

That's why it is so important to check over everything connected to your bow and arrow set-up to make sure it is all in A-1 shape before leaving the house. The time to do this is well before the season, so any repairs or replacements can be made in time to hunt.

3. PASSING THE FIRST GOOD SHOT

You spot a deer heading for your stand, and do the mental math: "OK, if he keeps coming, he'll get to that spot 20 yards out and I can smash him."

You pass up a 30-yard broadside shot, and maybe that quartering-away shot at 25 yards. Then, before the deer comes closer, something happens. He changes course. Another deer appears and draws him behind brush too thick to shoot through. Or, even worse, he gets to 15 yards and his radar finds you as you start to draw. All these, and more, have cost me deer of all shapes and sizes.

Now I have two basic rules when it comes to when to shoot: No. 1 is to take the first good shot a deer gives me within 35 yards. No. 2 is do not let a deer get closer than 20 yards.

4. POOR SHOOTING FORM

To shoot a consistently precise arrow, archers must maintain proper shooting form — regardless of the situation. That means keeping your bow arm's elbow slightly bent, your anchor point the same every time, and bending at the waist when shooting downhill. This form must be maintained even if you are required to twist your torso at an odd angle to take a shot at a deer that is off to the side or even directly behind your stand. You might have to rotate at the torso and bend or lean to clear limbs. To be able to do this, you must practice it.

It is imperative to practice shooting the same way you'll be hunting. That means from an elevated platform if you hunt from a tree stand, or from a stool if you hunt from a ground blind. It means putting on big, bulky hunting clothes — including your tree stand safety harness — and practicing reaching up and getting your bow off the hook, attaching your release, drawing, picking a spot, aiming and making the shot.

5. LOSS OF CONCENTRATION

The best deer hunters I know can multi-task with ease. When they decide it's time to shoot something, they have the ability to make things slow down in their minds. While focusing on the target animal, they also know where all the other deer are and what those animals are doing. They anticipate what is going to happen, and thus are able to know precisely when to draw and release. They pick a spot on the deer's chest and burn a hole through it with their eyes as they aim. They concentrate on follow-through, not allowing their bow arm to drop away too quickly.

NEVER MISS AGAIN?

Misses are part of archery. However, eliminate these five gaffes from your game, and chances are good you'll be eating backstrap this year, and not tag soup. ■

chapter 5

SHOOT A HEAVY ARROW

▶ MODERN COMPOUND BOWS HAVE EVOLVED into such well-designed and highly-efficient machines that models from every major manufacturer are capable of launching hunting arrows at speeds most of us only dreamed about a decade ago.

So why is it, then, that every time I turn on a hunting show, I see some big-name bowhunter shoot a whitetail and not achieve a complete pass-through on the animal?

This amazes me, because unless you smack a scapula, there is no reason to not blow a hunting shaft clean through the chest of even the largest whitetail at the ranges most deer are taken at.

Perhaps the reason is that many hunters are choosing arrows better suited to target shooting than killing a deer.

MEASURING ARROW ENERGY

Kinetic energy is an important part of the arrow penetration equation, though it is certainly not the entire story.

To calculate how much initial kinetic energy your arrows have, you need to know two things — how much your arrow shaft weighs (including fletching and broadhead) and how fast the arrow leaves the bow.

I weigh my arrows with the same electronic scale I use to weigh gunpowder when I'm reloading. Then, I simply shoot them through a chronograph to record the speed. Next, I plug the numbers into the standard kinetic energy formula — which is mass times velocity2, divided by 450,240. The result is the K.E. of your arrow in foot-pounds.

For example, my bow is set at 72 pounds. My 28½-inch shafts tipped with 100-grain broadheads weigh 401 grains. The initial arrow speed is choronographed one foot in front of the bow's riser. In this case, it is 284 fps. Plugging the numbers into the formula gives me an initial K.E. of 71.84 foot-pounds.

This is a lot of "juice" — way more than most experts believe is the minimum for deer-sized game. Minimum K.E. has been debated around archery circles for decades, but most people I respect have settled on a number somewhere near 50 foot-pounds. for whitetail-sized game.

You must remember, though, because arrows decelerate rather quickly as they travel downrange, the amount of K.E. delivered on target will be much less than initially generated at the shot. That's why an arrow that will blow right through a deer at 20 yards might only penetrate about half the shaft length at 40 yards.

GAINING MOMENTUM

Kinetic energy is far from the end-all determinant in penetration. If it were, bowhunters would be shooting arrow shafts that were light as a feather, because speed is twice as important as mass in the K.E. equation.

But in hunting, one other key scientific principle is also important — momentum.

Momentum is defined as "a property of a moving body that determines the length of time required to bring it to rest when under the action of a constant force."

One reason we hear little about momentum when talking about "bow power" is that it is too complicated for us to calculate without

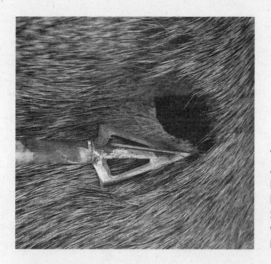

The other factor that seriously affects arrow penetration has nothing to do with bow kinetic energy or momentum. Simply put, razor-sharp blades will penetrate much more easily than dull blades.

having PhDs in mathematics. But really, all you need to know about momentum is that, all things being equal, heavier and denser objects traveling at the same speed as lighter objects will have greater momentum. Putting it another way, it is more difficult to stop a heavy arrow, which means it will penetrate more deeply.

THE TRAJECTORY FACTOR

The big reason many bowhunters choose light arrows is so they can get the most initial arrow speed possible out of their set-up. Some want to be able to brag to their buddies about what a screamer their set-up is. Others are looking for a flatter arrow trajectory.

However, lighter arrows shed arrow speed much faster as they travel downrange than heavier shafts do. Thus, when they arrive on target, they will have much less K.E. and much less momentum than arrows weighing more.

In addition, the average deer taken from a tree stand is killed at less than 25 yards. Trajectory isn't much of an issue.

If the deer is farther away, a laser rangefinder will tell you the distance. Therefore, a sloping trajectory isn't a problem.

Also keep in mind that the faster your set-up is, the more it will react to imperfections in shooting form and poor tuning.

DON'T FORGET THE TIP

There is another factor that seriously impacts penetration that has nothing to do with K.E. or momentum — the broadhead blades.

It's simple: Broadheads with scalpel-sharp blades slice through hair, hide, muscle and internal organs much easier than dull blades.

No matter how much poundage you pull, or how heavy or light your arrows are, you must hunt with broadheads that are so sharp they scare you. Dull blades will ensure poor penetration.

Team a razor-sharp head with even a moderately heavy arrow, and you are just about guaranteed a pass-through on a whitetail at an average range.

PUT ON A LITTLE WEIGHT

There are many reasons to choose moderately-heavy arrows instead of light shafts for bowhunting. The added weight helps soak up vibration and noise from the bow. The weight also gives the shaft more downrange momentum, a key factor in penetration. Plus, heavy shafts are more stable in the wind and deliver some fixed-blade broadheads with more accuracy.

Bowhunters with an average draw length — between 27 and 29 inches — and who shoot a minimum draw weight of 60 to 65 pounds should have no trouble achieving 50 ft./lbs of kinetic energy.

Even a 350-grain arrow leaving the bow at 250 fps has an initial K.E. of 45.2 foot-pounds. However, upping the arrow weight 25 grains — which can be accomplished by switching from a 100- to 125-grain broadhead — produces an initial K.E. of 52 foot-pounds, as well as more momentum downrange.

Switching to a heavier broadhead allows hunters to increase the weight of their current hunting arrows without purchasing new shafts. ∎

chapter 6

TUNING EXPANDABLE BROADHEADS

▶ I FEEL SO STRONGLY ABOUT PRACTICING with the exact same broadheads I hunt with that, for many years, I refused to hunt with expandable heads simply because the models I liked best utilized a rubber band to hold the blades in place. When I shot them into a target, the rubber band shredded, and I could never find replacements. So I didn't practice with them, and, therefore, didn't hunt with them. I used replaceable-blade heads that made it easy to practice with the real thing, then quickly and easily change out the blades when it was time to go hunting.

Today, many expandables come with a "practice head," which the manufacturer claims will fly exactly like the real thing. All you have to do is practice with one of these points, they say, and when hunting season rolls around, trade them out for a real broadhead. All is well.

That hasn't worked for me. I've tried a lot of these practice heads and have yet to find one that, for me, shoots into the same hole as a real broadhead.

As a caveat, I am a fanatical bow tuner. And unless my broadheads are giving me a perfect bullet-hole tear in paper at 10 yards, I will not go hunting — no exceptions. I've tried tuning expandable broadheads and the practice points, and they do not tear the same

for me. Ever.

Close? Sometimes.

The same? Nope.

I have tried all sorts of fixes to allow me to be able to practice with a real mechanical head.

When shooting expandables, the author will not settle for shooting the specialty practice points that come with new heads. Instead, he uses the real thing, and uses Scotch® tape to keep the blades from deploying.

A little dab of Super Glue® to hold the blades in place? It works for a shot or two, but then the glue breaks and the blades get covered with target gunk and I can't reglue it.

I know. This is probably a lot of nitpicking, and I have been told I am way too fanatical about these little things before. But having a mild dose of attention deficit disorder, I just can't help myself. I work too hard to get into position for a shot and know I can control my equipment and how it functions. I cannot predict or control what a mature buck will do.

SO SIMPLE IT'S STUPID

I was whining about this problem to a good friend, Jim Velasquez, this spring. He has been in the archery business more than 40 years, and is a crack shot. He's a superb bow tuner who used to own a quiver company and now works part-time in an archery pro shop while doing public relations for several archery companies.

"I can fix that for you," Jim said.

"What I do is trim a small strip of Scotch® tape and wrap it around the ferrule where the rubber band goes. The tape weighs about the same as the little rubber band and doesn't change the flight characteristics of the broadhead at all. Give it a try and see what you think."

So I did, and you know what?

It works like a charm.

The width of the tape is actually a perfect one-wrap fit around the ferrule, making it easy to trim a piece to fit.

It only lasts one shot, but I actually like that. It forces me to take my time between practice shots instead of just launching arrows as fast as I can shoot them — a very bad practice habit.

I did a fair amount of practicing this summer at longer ranges (40 to 80 yards) to see how the arrows fly when I taped the ferrule. The answer? The same as

TODAY, MANY EXPANDABLES COME WITH A "PRACTICE HEAD," WHICH THE MANUFACTURER CLAIMS WILL FLY EXACTLY LIKE THE REAL THING...I'VE TRIED A LOT OF THESE PRACTICE HEADS AND HAVE YET TO FIND ONE THAT, FOR ME, SHOOTS INTO THE SAME HOLE AS A REAL BROADHEAD.

when I use the rubber band.

The Swhacker broadheads I used employ two blades that fold backward, meaning I tape the ferrule in front of the blade assembly when using them.

It is a bit more complicated when using a slip-cam broadhead like the Rage, but you can make it work with them, too. It just takes a bit more finagling and a little more time. ∎

chapter 7

BROADHEAD TARGETS: SHOOT LIKE YOU HUNT

▶ I NEVER GAVE ARCHERY TARGETS much thought until I began shooting broadheads almost exclusively. When you shoot as much as I do, you quickly realize that you need a top-notch target that can take a lot of hits with a replaceable-blade broadhead. Yet, you would prefer to not require the strength of Hercules to remove your arrows.

Like most archers, I do my initial paper tuning with field points. And if it is months before hunting season, I will practice with the field tips using a standard bag-type target. However, when hunting seasons are a couple months away, I tune the bow again using the same broadheads I will be hunting with. After I get it perfect, I reset the sight pins and start shooting broadheads exclusively.

Thirty years ago, I hunted mostly with heavy fixed-blade broadheads made from steel. I shot them into a big sand bank for practice. Then, I simply re-sharpened the blades and went hunting. Today's aluminum ferrule broadheads are not really meant for sand bank shooting, thus the need for a broadhead target.

The first targets designed for modern broadheads were a pain. Most were made from a heavy plastic material that could take a lot of hits, but removing arrows was akin to trying to remove the mythical

THE FIRST TARGETS DESIGNED FOR MODERN BROADHEADS WERE MADE FROM A HEAVY PLASTIC MATERIAL THAT COULD TAKE A LOT OF HITS, BUT REMOVING ARROWS WAS AKIN TO TRYING TO REMOVE THE MYTHICAL *SWORD IN THE STONE* WITHOUT ROYAL BLOOD.

Sword in the Stone without royal blood. I can remember having to lay some targets on their side and stand on them to be able to get my arrows out. And after I started shooting fast carbon shafts, forget it. Sometimes so much heat was generated from the friction of the arrow entering the target it would melt and stick to the shaft!

Of course, the industry responded. New designs and materials created targets with longer life and easier arrow removal. However, some are more durable than others, especially when the archer is shooting broadheads.

"For an ethical bowhunter, target practice is of paramount importance," said Mike Weinkauf of Field Logic, makers of The Block and PolyFusion targets. "Trying to shoot out a broadhead target every year is an excellent goal. What archers need to realize is that not all targets are created equal.

"Our testing shows that some of today's most popular targets will have a pass-through failure with field points in less than 1,000 shots. If you're practicing with broadheads, your target may not last half that long before you experience a pass-through."

Early broadhead targets that permitted any semblance of easy arrow extraction frustrated all of us with their lack of durability. How-

ever, archers must also realize that when shooting a fast arrow tipped with a razor blade into any target, that target will get shredded over time. It is completely unrealistic to think a broadhead target will last as long as a bag-type target shot with nothing but field points. Still, the best self-healing

A small broadhead target can be packed for hunting camp, allowing archers to make sure their sights are on and shooting skills honed during a hunt. However, having a larger target at home will extend its life, especially if you don't just shoot the center.

broadhead targets out there will withstand a lot of hits as well as bad weather should they be left outdoors for a prolonged period.

To help increase the durability of your broadhead targets regardless of make or model, here are a couple of tips. First, buy the biggest target you can both afford and transport. The larger the target, the larger the surface area to shoot, which will translate into longer life.

Second, targets that permit shooting on four sides will last longer than those that can be shot on only one or two sides.

Third, and perhaps most important, do not shoot only at the center of the target. To achieve maximum target life, you have to spread the hits around. To help me do this without the risk of missing the target entirely, I shoot the center of my targets when getting my sight pins set. Then I shoot at spots scattered around the edges of the target at reasonable distances (for me that is to about 50 yards), saving the center for long-range shooting where a greater margin of error is needed.

What about 3D targets?

I love shooting life-like targets, especially when replicating actual hunting conditions, such as when practicing shooting from either a tree stand or ground blind. For maximum life, there are targets with a replaceable vital area core.

Good broadhead targets can cost as little as $50 to as much as $200. However, they are worth the investment.

I personally like to have two: one larger premium model I keep at home, and a smaller, less expensive model that's easily-transportable in my truck that goes with me to hunting camp. ■

chapter 8

FIELD REPAIRS CAN SAVE YOUR HUNT

▶ IT WAS THE FIRST DAY of a long-awaited rut hunt. I was hunting on a farm known for producing big bucks, and I was so pumped I barely slept a wink. An hour before first light I climbed into my stand, secured my safety belt, and began hauling my bow up. I had it three feet from the platform when, to my horror, the pull rope came untied and the bow went crashing to the ground. I climbed down to find my sight was completely trashed. Two of my five pins were broken, and the housing was bent.

My pricey week-long guided hunt could have been all over before it even started ... except I was prepared. I radioed my guide, who came and picked me up. Back at the lodge, I dug into my bow case and pulled out my spare sight, attached it, and then went out to check the zero. I was back up a different tree just three hours later.

MURPHY'S LAW

There is no doubt in my mind that the infamous Murphy of Murphy's Law was a diehard archer. Modern compound bows and their accessories are intricate tools with parts that take constant pampering just to keep them in tune and properly sighted in. There is not an experienced bowhunter that, at some time, has not been bitten in the

Quick Fixes for Common Problems

Peep sight: Peep sights can slide up and down the bowstring, so mark the peep's location on the string with an indelible marker. If you use a peep that requires rubber tubing to align it at full draw, be aware that this tubing will deteriorate pretty quickly. Check it constantly and always carry a spare. Tubeless peeps are prone to not aligning perfectly unless you give them a slight twist before you draw, so don't forget!

Bow sight: The best advice anyone can give you is to use the toughest bow sight you can buy with the least amount of moving parts, a rugged pin guard, and strong, protected fiber-optic pins. Use an indelible marker to mark your vertical and horizontal adjustments of the sight pin housing, and constantly check all screws for tightness.

Arrow rest: These are absolutely the biggest bugaboo on your bow. After the bow is tuned, use your marker to mark the horizontal and vertical adjustments, and check the tightness of all mounting screws often. Make sure you pad rest prongs and the bow's riser with stick-on moleskin.

Bow-string: If the string fails you're done. One time I was hunting mountain lions in Montana and I slipped and fell during a hike along an icy creek in a snow squall. My bow went flying. When I picked it up I saw the string had come off the cams! Thankfully I had a backup bow. Later, I was able to take the damaged bow to a local pro shop and get the thing put back together. If you don't have a spare bow, you need a spare bowstring, loop material, nock sets, string wax, and a portable press and know how to replace it exactly the way the original was.

Release: Quality is critical. Check for debris that can sneak its way into the moving parts area and keep it lubricated. Also check the jaws for nicks and the wrist strap for wear and fraying (I had an old strap snap on me during a hunt.) Always carry a spare.

behind by some sort of equipment malfunction. It's not a big deal if it happens at home or on the practice range. It's a different story in hunting camp, especially if you are in a remote camp or hunting in rural America where the nearest archery pro shop is 100 miles away.

You need to be able to solve any problems that occur mid-hunt by yourself. The best way to do this is to anticipate anything that can go wrong — everything — and take preventative measures before leaving home.

I have learned about lots of these issues simply because I have played with lots of bows and accessories over a lot of years. One thing I have learned is that you should never trust a hunt to an untested piece of equipment — whether it's an arrow rest, bow sight, peep sight or release aid.

> ONE THING I HAVE LEARNED IS THAT YOU SHOULD NEVER TRUST A HUNT TO AN UNTESTED PIECE OF EQUIPMENT — WHETHER IT'S AN ARROW REST, BOW SIGHT, PEEP SIGHT OR RELEASE AID.

Recently, I was in Quebec with the new Hoyt Carbon Matrix bow. I had a drop-away rest on it, but when I got to camp and took some practice shots I saw the cord that pulls the launcher arms up was fraying on a slight imperfection in the rest housing. Fortunately, I had a spare piece of the right-sized cord in my traveling tool kit and was able to make a hasty repair. Had I not been prepared, though, my hunt would have been in jeopardy.

AN OUNCE OF PREVENTION

You can prevent a lot of problems with your bow's accessories, at least in part, by selecting only time-tested designs with the fewest moving parts and bomb-proof construction.

Then, after you've assembled the bow, look at every part and try to visualize anything that might go wrong and learn how to fix them.

Here's what I do now when traveling any distance from home:

First, I have two bows all set up, tuned, sighted in and ready to hunt. If my No. 1 bow goes down for any reason, I simply grab No. 2 and get back after it.

I also have a little spare parts kit that goes with me everywhere. It has everything from spare screws and rest parts to a tube of super glue. Other necessities include string serving material, nock sets, string loop material, a roll of electrician's tape, extra peeps and a string separator.

I also travel with a spare release aid and complete set of Allen wrenches. About the only camp repair I cannot make is replacing a bowstring. But since I have a spare bow, that doesn't bother me much. I also bring a soft bow case along to protect my bow when traveling in a truck or on an ATV.

This might sound like paranoia to some — except Murphy, who is always waiting. ■

chapter 9

CRAFT SHOOTING LANES FOR SUCCESS

▶ A DECADE AGO, I was doing a lot of filming for cable television hunting shows. Fortunately, one of the cameramen I worked with, Chuck Jones, was a stone-cold killer. He knew how to film, and he knew how to find deer and pick good trees. We made a pretty efficient team in the deer woods.

Unlike a lot of the guys I hunt with, Jones was not afraid to trim limbs. He even cut down small-diameter trees to create shooting lanes. His philosophy was simple: What good does it do if a deer walks within range and we can't shoot it?

I've also hunted with guys who believe that the only way you'll ever get a shot at a mature buck is to never trim a thing. Their theory is also simple: Mature bucks know their core areas like you know your living room. Rearranging the furniture will tip them off that something is amiss, which will make them that much harder to kill.

Which theory is right?

Probably both of them.

Many deer hunters fail to consider shooting lanes when selecting a specific tree to hang a stand in. However, along with wind direction and sun position, shooting lanes are one of my primary considerations in choosing a tree. The ideal tree provides ease of move-

ment and many natural shooting lanes, while still providing enough natural cover and a good backdrop to keep me hidden.

Clear lanes to be able to maneuver and shoot your bow, but still leave enough branches and leaves surrounding you in the stand to break up your outline and keep you hidden.

Not leaving enough cover in and around the stand is one of the biggest mistakes a tree-stand hunter makes. However, you can also handicap yourself with too much cover.

TIMING AND LOCATION MATTER

In a perfect world, you are able to scout your hunting ground and select a handful of ambush spots well ahead of hunting season. You can trim shooting lanes months ahead of time, allowing any local deer to get used to your handiwork. Still, by the time hunting season arrives, limbs and leaves have grown out, requiring a minimal amount of pruning to re-open the shooting lanes. That is why I make sure I always have a set of pruning shears and a small hand saw in my backpack.

Summer cutting can be more substantial than last-minute pruning. Large limbs and even entire trees can be taken out with enough time before hunting season that the deer can get comfortable again. However, some new research on mature white-tailed bucks suggests that any encroachment into their core areas can, and often does, send them packing — often for good. This research suggests that a hunter should never encroach on a buck's core area, even in the off-season. It reinforces something I have long believed: A serious big buck hunter must be cognizant of his impact on deer 24/7, 365. For me, that means not going on summer treks to the woods to start cutting down trees unless I am doing so in places other than core bedding areas.

Travel corridors, field edges and along water courses? Fine. Bedding thickets? I never, ever, go near them.

NO LEAD TIME

I hunt lots of places each fall, so I often find myself scouting on-the-go — which means I set new stands during hunting season a lot. When I do, I try to keep my trimming to a minimum. Yet, I also recognize that unless I can slip my arrow through the junk, I might as well be watching TV. Each location and situation is different, so prudence and common sense come into play.

NOT LEAVING ENOUGH COVER IN AND AROUND THE STAND IS ONE OF THE BIGGEST MISTAKES A TREE-STAND HUNTER MAKES. HOWEVER, YOU CAN ALSO HANDICAP YOURSELF WITH TOO MUCH COVER.

Time of year can be one factor I weigh. If I am trimming an early-season stand leading to a food plot, for example, I will keep trimming to a minimum because I assume any shot I get will be at a deer walking down the trail I am set up on. During the rut, when deer are chasing each other willy-nilly and I'm set up in a funnel, I want to be able to extend my shooting range. Plus, I assume that trimming and cutting will have less effect on deer.

OTHER CONSIDERATIONS

One mistake many hunters make is not opening up shooting lanes that permit shots at extended distances. Sure, you want to shoot your buck at 20 paces, but what if it walks past at 30? I am comfortable with my bow at that range, and I want to be able to make that shot.

If you hunt public land, it might also be crucial to disguise your shooting lanes to keep others from knowing where your stands are. There is nothing like freshly cut limbs and tree trunks to give a spot away. I always remove trimmed limbs, erase footprints, and even go so far as to rub mud and dirt on the surfaces of freshly cut trunks to keep them from being noticed by man or deer.

IN THE END

The bottom line is that you need clear lanes to be able to maneuver and shoot your bow, while still having enough branches and leaves surrounding you in the stand to break up your outline and keep you hidden. Find that balance, and you'll find more success. ■

chapter 10

NO EXCUSES: WEAR A HARNESS EVERY TIME!

"On Saturday, November 1, 2008, Brian C. Aldridge, age 38 of Butler, died as the result of injuries received in a tree stand accident on the opening day of Tennessee's muzzleloader season. Aldridge was found approximately 100 yards from a tree from which he had fallen."
— **Tennessee Wildlife Resources Agency**

▶ NATIONAL STUDIES CONDUCTED by *Deer & Deer Hunting Magazine* indicate that approximately 33 percent of hunters who hunt from an elevated stand will have an incident sometime in their hunting career. Some will not live to tell their story. Others will tell it from a hospital bed or wheelchair. Many accident victims will never hunt again. The scary part is that these accidents can be avoided.

Some states report higher fatality rates associated with tree stand incidents than with firearm incidents. A 2006 study commissioned by the Consumer Product Safety Commission showed that the average age of the victims who fell or hung to their death is 44 years old. These are hunters with up to 20 years of experience who, like many of us, got lazy and too familiar with the risks. Yet, in 75 percent of the deaths, the subject was not wearing a full body harness.

One hunter who fell and lived to tell about it is John Wydner.

During a Michigan deer hunt in 2000, Wydner found his tree stand crashing to the rocks below and himself clinging to the tree for his life.

Sliding down a bark-covered trunk left the terrified hunter bloodied and shaken. All he could do was think about how close he had just come to severe injury or death. That night back at camp John, brother Jerry and hunting buddy Jim Barta put their heads together to try and figure out a way to make a safety harness easy to put on and comfortable to wear. A truckload of ideas and prototypes later, Hunter Safety Systems was born.

Yet, when Jerry Wydner shared that story with me at a business meeting in Spring 2009, it reminded me of how lax I have been at

Top Choices for Full-Body Harnesses

A variety of easy to use full-body harnesses are available today. Here are some top options and contact information.

Ameristep
The Climbing Vest Harness
www.ameristep.com

Gorilla
EXO Tech Safety Harness
www.gorillatreestands.com

Hunter Safety Systems
The Pro Series HSS-6
and Treestalker HSS-7
www.huntersafetysystem.com

Muddy Outdoors
Safeguard Series
www.muddyoutdoors.com

Summit
Seat-O-the-Pants
www.summittsands.com

Trophyline USA
ArmourLite Safety Harness
www.trophylineusa.com

Mountaineer Sports
Rescue One Controlled Decent System
www.mountaineer-sports.com

times hunting from elevated stands. I mean, I'm a professional, right? This stuff always happens to somebody else. Right?

Today's safety harnesses are a snap to get on and off — easily fitting over your outermost layer after you reach your stand. They're fully adjustable and quiet, and have additional features like pockets and built-in deer drags.

Wrong.

A decade ago, hunters like me justified not wearing a safety harness for several reasons. The harnesses and safety belts of the day were horribly uncomfortable, a pain in the petunias to put on and take off, and often got in the way when we tried to draw and aim our bows.

I still remember a monster Kansas buck that kept his scalp when I had to spin in my tree to draw on him and my old harness made that maneuver completely impossible.

Man, was I ticked off!

But today, there are several companies that offer excellent full-body safety harnesses designed specifically for stand hunting.

They're a snap to get on and off — easily fitting over your outermost layer after you reach your stand. They're fully adjustable and quiet, and have additional features like pockets and built-in deer drags.

I know times are hard for a lot of us. Money is tight. But if you are a serious deer hunter, the best investment you'll ever make is a top-quality full-body harness. ■

chapter 11

QUIT SHIVERING AND MAKE THE SHOT

▶   THE FIRST TIME I sat in a tree stand when the temperature fell below freezing, I couldn't believe my troubles. My bow — always a good friend — became stiff and gruff. Plus, I was too cold to sit without dancing. I don't doubt every deer in the county knew where I was long before they came into range.

Extreme cold weather can take a toll on both your body and equipment. Therefore, you have to make some modifications in both your equipment and your preparations if you want to be able to shoot an accurate arrow in bitter weather.

KEEPING WARM AND DRY

It is imperative you stay warm as toast to be able to both sit still for hours in bitter weather, then make the shot when the opportunity arises. That means fueling the body, then dressing properly.

A solid breakfast built around carbohydrates that can be easily digested and turned into body heat is important. I like pancakes and peanut butter toast, food that will stick with me all day. My pack contains chewy granola bars and a sandwich for lunchtime. A thermos of hot chocolate helps, too, but I also bring water to prevent dehydration.

It is critical to wear undergarments made from synthetic materials — not cotton — that will wick sweat off your body and into the next layer of clothing, negating convective heat loss that will chill you to the bone.

A bulky jacket can interfere with bowstring travel during the shot. Wearing a full-length arm guard will help keep your sleeve off the string.

Blocking the wind is also crucial to your comfort and efficiency as a bowhunter. I wear fleece or other synthetic outerwear featuring either a Gore-Tex or Gore Windstopper membrane. Both membranes breathe to let moisture vapor out away from the body, yet they also block 100 percent of the wind. Wearing an upper and lower body garment with these membranes allows me to wear less total layers, so it's easier to shoot my bow without fear of a shot-destroying bowstring-clothing collision.

Don't overlook your head, feet and hands. Wear warm pac-type boots and wicking socks. It's impossible to shoot well with bulky gloves on, so I wear only a light pair of gloves. I keep my hands warm by wearing an insulated muff around my waist that I can stick my hands in. In the muff I keep a HeatMax disposable chemical hand-warmer. I've used this system in weather as cold as minus 30 degrees.

Remember a bulky jacket can interfere with bowstring travel during the shot. Wearing a full-length arm guard will help keep your sleeve off the string. So will an archery chest protector. A bino system also compresses my jacket and keeps it away from my string.

BOW MODIFICATIONS

You might be Hercules and easily draw a 70-pound bow during early seasons. However, when cold weather comes, the combination of stiff muscles and extra clothing makes it difficult to smoothly draw the same bow. I like to crank my draw weight down 10 percent for bitter-weather hunts. When you turn the bow down, remember that you have to re-tune it until it is shooting bullet holes through paper — which might mean changing to an arrow with a different spine — and then reset your sight pins.

I also re-lubricate my bow's moving parts with a graphite or synthetic product. I use the same stuff on my release aid. Bows with wood or plastic grips are preferred in cold weather over bare metal grips. Wrap the grip with tape, leather or foam for warmth.

It is also a good idea to hang your bow from a hook attached to either the tree or your tree

YOU MIGHT BE HERCULES AND EASILY DRAW A 70-POUND BOW DURING EARLY SEASONS. HOWEVER, WHEN COLD WEATHER COMES, STIFF MUSCLES AND EXTRA CLOTHING MAKE IT DIFFICULT TO SMOOTHLY DRAW THE SAME BOW.

stand. Holding an ice-cold metal bow riser in your hands will chill them rapidly.

If you use a peep sight, be sure to constantly check it for ice. One time, I had some snow fall from an overhanging limb onto my bow. Thinking nothing of it, I brushed it away and resumed my vigil. When a deer finally showed and I came to full draw, I found snow had gotten into my peep sight and frozen. I couldn't see a thing, and had to pass the shot until I could clear the peep.

You might need to slightly modify your shooting form, too. To avoid catching your string, try opening up your stance a bit and facing the target a little more directly than usual. This will help get your arms away from your body. Be sure to practice with your cold-weather clothes on before your hunt to see what kind of tweaking must be made.

TREE STAND SQUEAKS

Tree stands are notorious for squeaking and groaning in cold weather. Two things will help. The first is to re-lubricate moving parts and chains with the same synthetic lubricant you use on your bow. The second is to simply re-hang the stand snugly against the tree trunk to prevent subtle movements.

Pad the stand floor with an old piece of carpet to prevent your feet from making noise when you shuffle them about. If you leave it overnight, turn it over or store it in a plastic bag to prevent ice. I cover my stand seat with a bag overnight for the same reason.

I've killed bucks in temperatures well below zero. The key is to remember that bowhunting bitter weather is different from the early season. Eat well, dress properly, and modify your bow. You, too, will enjoy hot hunting during the coldest days of the year. ■

chapter 12

GUIDE YOUR TARGET FOR BETTER SHOTS

▶ FOR A LONG TIME, I looked at fences on hunting land as a real pain. All they seemed to do was hold up gates I had to keep opening and closing, or rip my pants and shirts when I tried to go over them.

Then I began talking with landowners about fences, and how they might be used as a positive in my deer hunting. Today, my attitude has changed. I still hate to open and close gates, but I have learned that fences can be a real tool in an archer's war chest.

FENCE CROSSINGS

Fences are nothing more than man-made boundaries. They mark property lines, as well as help section off land into various different uses. They keep cattle, horses and other large domestic animals confined to certain areas and, more importantly, out of others.

Fences can serve other functions, too, and they aren't all made from wire and steel posts. For example, rock walls can help shore up creek banks and water holes. And when woods are cleared, the resulting detritus can be pushed up to form a barrier along field edges.

All types of fence barriers can be used to your advantage when bow hunting. The most obvious is to locate trails that indicate places where deer frequently cross a fence. Depending on conditions and the time of year, these fence crossings can be excellent places to set a stand.

Spots where deer are crossing under a fence are easy to see. Just look for a well-worn trail, then check the lower strand of fence for deer hair. Soft, pliable hair coupled with fresh tracks is the kind of sign even a blind man can interpret.

You can take this a step further by scouting to find where the deer crossing the fence are coming from and going to. I arrowed a nice 8-point buck one year in Kansas hunting such a set-up. The fence ran across an oak-studded hill. On one side was a large, brush-choked flat that deer used as a bedding thicket. On the other side was a 5-acre green field and small cluster of white oak trees that were dropping a load of large, sweet nuts. Walking the fence, I found where the deer were obviously crossing under it in two places. However, I set up away from those spots, on a less well-defined trail. This trail had a rub line running along it, and where it met the fence the top strand of the four-foot high fence hung low. If you looked closely you could see where a buck or two traveled up the trail along the rub line, jumped the fence, and headed down the slope to check the field for does.

WITH SOME CAREFUL THOUGHT AND ANALYSIS, MOST FENCES CAN BE USED TO THE BOW HUNTER'S ADVANTAGE. START LOOKING AT THEM AS YOUR ALLY, NOT YOUR ENEMY.

I used a climbing stand to set up in a big red oak just off the crest of the hill on the bedding thicket side of the fence, and gave myself a 25-yard shot to the fence crossing. The first afternoon, the buck came up out of the bottom like a submarine, passed right next to the 6-inch cedar he'd been rubbing, and approached the crossing spot. He never made it.

FENCING FOR FUNNELS

You can also use fences as artificial barriers that can produce shot opportunities that might otherwise not occur. One way is by pushing brush and downed trees into solid barriers around newly-created fields. My friend Chuck Sykes, a biologist who specializes in both creating top-quality deer programs for landowners as well as booking fee hunts on these well-managed properties showed me how this works near his Alabama home.

Sykes takes it to the extreme. He had used heavy equipment to clear a 3-acre food plot, which he subsequently planted in clover and alfalfa. As he cleared the land, he piled the slash along the field edge so it created a solid barrier on two sides of the field. Those sides just happened to be the ones that his scouting had shown were nearest the most commonly-used bedding thickets. Then, he strategically opened up two small holes in the wall right where two well-used trails ran.

ALL TYPES OF FENCE BARRIERS CAN BE USED TO YOUR ADVANTAGE WHEN BOW HUNTING. THE MOST OBVIOUS IS TO LOCATE TRAILS THAT INDICATE PLACES WHERE DEER FREQUENTLY CROSS A FENCE.

Both openings had large oaks within 25 yards — perfect for an archery ambush site. He also erected a shooting house across the field for gun hunters.

OPEN THE FLOOD GATES

Some fences are built so it is tough for deer to cross them. By making it easy for them to get from one side to the other you can often set up shots that you might not otherwise get.

For example, if you find a heavily-used trail that parallels a fence for any distance before crossing, you can sometimes encourage the deer to cross the fence at a place where it is to your advantage to set up a stand. With the landowner's permission, loosen and raise the lower fence strand between a pair of fence posts near a good stand location. This will create a duck-under where the deer have a more direct route to the food.

With some careful thought and analysis, most fences can be used to the bow hunter's advantage. Start looking at them as your ally, not your enemy. ■

chapter 13

BROADHEAD DESIGN: DOES IT MATTER?

▶ THERE IS NO END to the armchair theories I hear on the subject of broadhead penetration. However, it's safe to say that a well-matched bow-and-arrow combination that has been tuned with broadhead affixed will penetrate plenty deep to take deer-sized game regardless of the make, model or design of the broadhead. That's certain to raise hackles on many necks — and there are some caveats that need to be addressed — but it's a fair assessment of how far archery technology has come.

FOCUSED ENERGY

The first caveat is arrow flight, which can affect penetration significantly. With perfect arrow flight, all the stored energy in the arrow is placed directly behind the broadhead. However, if an arrow flies tail-left or tail-right, you might still hit where you aim, but some of the energy stored in the shaft will not directly aid in penetration.

This rationale, and accuracy issues, are the two reasons why you should never hunt with a bow-and-arrow set-up that is not perfectly tuned.

THE PHYSICS OF PENETRATION

Three major principles can be used to measure the penetration of a perfectly-tuned arrow. Kinetic energy (KE) is the most significant factor affecting arrow penetration, regardless of the style of broadhead. Calculate KE by totalling the velocity multiplied by the velocity multiplied by arrow weight then divided by 450,240. The accompanying chart shows the amount of KE arrow maker Easton Technical Products recommends for various categories of game. As you can see, it doesn't take much for bowhunting whitetails.

Related to KE is momentum — the tendency of an object in motion to remain in motion. All things being equal, heavier objects have more momentum than lighter objects. A 125-grain head, for example, helps carry more momentum than a 100-grain head.

The third factor is friction, which is the drag during penetration. Larger-diameter shafts will have more drag than smaller-diameter shafts. Broadhead design also increases or decreases friction. In the old days, friction was something of a penetration issue. However, it is a relatively insignificant factor with today's equipment.

BROADHEAD DESIGN: DOES IT MATTER?

This brings us to broadhead design. Discussions about which broadhead design penetrates best have been going on since the earliest days of bowhunting. I remember when it was two- versus three-

Kinetic Energy (KE) and Big Game Hunting

KE	Hunting Usage
<25 ft. lbs.	Small Game
25-41 ft. lbs.	Medium Game (deer, antelope, etc.)
42-65 ft. lbs.	Large Game (elk, black bear, wild boar, etc.)
>65 ft. lbs.	Toughest Game (cape buffalo, grizzly, etc.)

Modern compound bows, shooting well-matched medium-weight carbon shafts that are tuned perfectly, can run nearly any quality broadhead through the chest of a white-tailed deer.

blade heads. Next, it was cutting tip versus chisel point. Then it was standard ferrule length versus a short ferrule. Then, of course, came the debate between the penetrating abilities of fixed-blade heads versus mechanical heads. Within that is the debate among mechanical designs — the older, flip-open type (where the blades fold back along the ferrule upon impact) or the newer slip-cam design. Finally, with mechanicals the question has recently arisen about the penetrating abilities of heads with super-wide cutting diameters of 2½ inches or more.

Just a few years ago, all this would have been fodder for a good discussion. Today, the point is really moot. A good friend of mine did a pretty comprehensive broadhead penetration test with mechanical broadheads. While he found the best heads penetrated 22 percent deeper than the worst, pretty much all of them penetrated the testing media deeply enough for whitetail hunting. He also tested a popular replaceable-blade head as a control. This head out-penetrated all but four of the mechanicals. Yet, this test — plus the vast amount of information available from hunters — tells us the equipment available today makes every broadhead deadly.

For those still hunting with the compounds, arrow shafts and broadheads of yesteryear: You are way behind the curve when it comes to the accuracy and lethality of your bow-and-arrow set-up.

WHAT TO WORRY ABOUT

Modern compound bows, shooting well-matched medium-weight carbon shafts that are tuned perfectly, can run nearly any quality broadhead through the chest of a white-tailed deer. The broadhead can be of fixed, replaceable-blade or mechanical design. As long as the broadhead is sharp, it will do the job.

Of course, this assumes you do your part and place the shot where it needs to be placed. There certainly can be a significant difference in broadhead performance when you hit an animal in the wrong spot, such as a shoulder blade or leg bone. Yet, there is no real way to make any predictions about penetration from this type of hit. Every bad hit on an animal is a little different, and each broadhead performs a little differently depending upon the circumstances.

If you choose a broadhead with at least a 1-inch cutting diameter, your biggest concern should be keeping the blades sharp and putting it in the right spot. ■

chapter 14

IS YOUR BROADHEAD TOO LIGHT?

▶ IN THE 1970s AND EARLY 1980s, when compound bow design was primitive compared to today's standards, archers released heavy aluminum arrows with fingers. The shafts were tipped with either fixed-blade or replaceable-blade broadheads that commonly weighed between 125 and 150 grains. Such heavy heads were required to achieve the necessary weight-forward balance for straight and true arrow flight. A "hot" compound of the day produced initial arrow speeds of maybe 220 fps with an arrow shaft/broadhead combination that typically weighed between 500 and 600 grains.

Today, of course, most whitetail bowhunters shooting modern bows use an shaft/broadhead combination that weighs between 350 and 425 grains. And these bows are delivering an initial velocity of somewhere between 250 and 290 fps. Most of us are now shooting carbon arrows, which makes finding a shaft with the proper spine much easier than when using aluminum shafts. When the trend for lighter arrows started in the 1980s and early 1990s, the most popular broadhead size sold was 125 grains. Now the most common choice has dropped to 100 grains. In fact, some bowhunters, obsessed with raw arrow speed, are choosing heads that weigh as little as 75 grains.

Although our gear has certainly changed, the question is still a common one: How do I choose the proper broadhead weight for whitetail hunting?

SPEED ISN'T EVERYTHING

This issue is sometimes clouded by the marketing used to sell bows — much of which is based on the bow's IBO speed. Faster is better, right? And by using a lighter broadhead, you'll achieve faster arrow flight.

Yet, the average bow shooter will only gain somewhere between 4 to 8 fps in raw arrow speed by choosing a 100-grain head instead of one that weighs 125 grains. The flatter trajectory gained by this miniscule speed increase is almost negligible when taking shots at whitetails, because most come at under 35 yards.

Thus, the most important consideration in choosing between 100- and 125-grain heads should be maintaining a sufficient front-of-center balance of the assembled arrow shaft. Having enough FOC will improve stability in flight, which in turn will improve accuracy and give you a bit more momentum when the head begins driving through a deer's chest.

Most experts agree that an FOC of 10 to 15 percent is needed for optimum arrow flight. To determine your finished arrow's FOC, measure the shaft from the nock throat to the tip of the arrow shaft. Next, with broadhead installed, balance the shaft on the dull edge of a knife and

THE AVERAGE BOW SHOOTER WILL ONLY GAIN SOMEWHERE BETWEEN 4 TO 8 FPS IN RAW ARROW SPEED BY CHOOSING A 100-GRAIN HEAD INSTEAD OF ONE THAT WEIGHS 125 GRAINS.

mark the balance point with a pen. Measure from the nock's throat to the balance point.

Divide that number by the length of the overall arrow shaft. This will yield the decimal equivalent of the balance point's percentage of overall arrow length. Subtract .50, move the decimal two places to the right and you have your arrow shaft's percent of FOC.

Today most whitetail bow-hunters shooting modern bows use an shaft/broadhead combination that weighs between 350 and 425 grains, delivering an initial velocity of somewhere between 250 and 290 fps.

BEEFING UP

If you measure your current shaft's FOC using your favorite 100-grain broadhead, you might be surprised to find it is either inadequate or marginal. If that is the case, to achieve optimal arrow flight and penetration you'll need to either reduce the weight of the rear of the shaft, add weight to the front of the shaft — or a little of both.

Remember, too, that using a heavier or lighter broadhead will affect the dynamic spine of the arrow. When you add more weight to the front of the shaft, the spine is actually reduced a bit. Using a lighter broadhead will increase the spine a little. Conversely, adding more weight to the rear of the shaft will increase arrow spine, while subtracting weight from the rear will decrease spine.

Adjusting the rear is most commonly accomplished with heavier or lighter fletches, but adding wraps, cresting or illuminated nocks will also add weight to the rear of the shaft.

ACCURACY TRUMPS SPEED

There are, of course, other considerations besides weight when choosing broadheads for whitetail hunting. No. 1 on my list is the head's construction. I want stout ferrules and thick blades that are razor sharp. I also want tight manufacturing tolerances so the finished broadhead weight that is within +/- 5 grains of the advertised weight. I also want a minimum cutting diameter of 1⅛-inches.

Of course, I want to shoot the fastest hunting arrow I can shoot accurately for the flatter trajectory, increased kinetic energy and momentum. However, the most accurate arrow I can shoot is one with the proper spine and a more than adequate FOC.

If that means that I have to use a 125-grain broadhead and shoot 265 fps instead of 272 fps, so be it. Because when it is all said and done, accuracy — not raw arrow speed — is what it is all about. ■

chapter 15

SHORT BROADHEADS: PROS AND CONS

▶ FOR THE MOST PART, radical equipment changes to bows, arrows and accessories are slow in coming. The sport is steeped in tradition, and archers tend to stick with the tried-and-true. For example, the new world of drop-away arrow rests has proven that they help the average archer's ability to make the shot, yet most bowhunters still have not given one a serious look.

It is the business end of a hunting arrow that has brought about some of the most controversial changes. Mechanical broadheads have been around for more than a decade, yet the debate over their effectiveness remains heated and, in fact, they remain illegal in some states. The latest buzz centers on a new generation of short broadheads. These replaceable-blade heads look just like the traditional three-blade replaceable-blade heads they mimic, the difference being they are smaller all-around than their standard-sized counterparts. They have shorter ferrules, smaller blades and slightly smaller cutting diameters. Several reputable manufacturers are selling them, and they have enough momentum to seriously affect the marketplace for years to come.

It's all about aerodynamics. Basically, broadheads with the largest exposed blade surface area are affected by wind and air flow more

The Sonic Pro 100 is just one of several short broadhead designs.

than broadheads with smaller exposed blade surface areas. The larger heads, therefore, have a greater tendency to steer the arrow shaft. Known as "planing," this can occur when shooting a well-tuned bow in a medium to stiff crosswind, when shooting a bow-and-arrow combination that is slightly out of tune, or when a broadhead is screwed into the shaft and is slightly misaligned. (All these scenarios occur more often than many archers suspect.)

Mechanical broadheads are popular with many bowhunters for two reasons. Depending on the design, they can offer huge cutting diameters once their blades fold out, and they also have little or no exposed blade surfaces to catch the wind. Why is this important? Super high-speed photography of a bow being shot shows that even arrow shafts affixed with helical fletches do not rotate much until they are well off the bowstring. This means that, except for the most perfect of conditions, if the arrow isn't rotating it is susceptible to planing. When the fletching begins to aggressively spin the shaft through the air, planing is reduced or eliminated and the shaft flies straight and true. Simply stated, all broadheads with exposed blade surfaces will plane to some degree or another. The more blade surface there is the more planing will occur, and the more critical precise bow tuning becomes. Thus, shorter broadheads with less exposed blade surface will plane less than their larger cousins.

The shorter ferrules of these next-generation broadheads require manufacturers to both shorten their blades to fit and change the angle of the blade as it sits on the ferrule. This does two things — it reduces the overall blade surface available to cut a hole in tissue, and the more severe angle requires more kinetic energy to force its way through that tissue than blades at a less severe angle. The latter point is a moot one, however, given that most modern compound bows set at all but the lightest of draw weights shooting all but the very lightest arrow shafts produce plenty of energy.

IF YOU ARE NOT A FAN OF MECHANICAL HEADS BUT WANT A BROADHEAD THAT WILL GIVE YOU THE VERY BEST ACCURACY FROM A FAST BOW, THIS NEW GENERATION OF SHORT BROADHEADS DESERVES YOUR ATTENTION.

The reduced cutting diameter issue, however, can be a factor. Virtually every broadhead maker I have spoken with about this topic said the same thing — the bigger hole you can cut in an animal, the better off you are. (This, by the way, is another strong selling point for those mechanical heads with cutting diameters of 2 inches or more.) The smaller hole produces less tissue damage and a leaner the blood trail, which is not a good thing. Most short heads have a cutting diameter between ⅞ and 1⅛ inches, while the average cutting diameter of standard-sized heads is 1⅛ to 1¼ inches.

The shorter, more compact ferrules of these new broadheads make them stronger than longer, standard heads. This means little when everything is perfect and the head zips through soft muscle and tissue. When it hits a solid object like bone, however, it becomes a factor. The shorter length of these new heads also allows the manufacturer to make it thicker than a comparable standard-sized head of the same weight, which adds to its strength. The same is true of blades. All things being equal, the shorter heads are the strongest.

Despite my preference for large cutting areas, I decided to give several of these new short heads (Rocket Ultimate Steel 100) a try the last couple seasons. One thing I really like about them is the fact they do fly extremely well. I have used them only on deer-sized game, and so far I have had no problems in terms of quickly letting the air out of anything I have hit.

If you are not a fan of mechanical heads but want a broadhead that will give you the very best accuracy from a fast bow, this new generation of short broadheads deserves your attention. They seem to work very well from fast compounds shooting arrows at speeds of 270 feet per second or more.

Keep in mind the compromises mentioned above, however, particularly the fact that they do not cut as large a hole as many standard-sized replaceable-blade heads. Check them out, then log on to deeranddeerhunting.com and let us know how they worked for you. ■

chapter 16

RANGEFINDERS: BEYOND THE BASICS

▶ IF YOU'RE A SERIOUS WHITETAIL HUNTER, you probably already own a laser rangefinder. If you do not, you need to put one on the top of your wish list.

It doesn't matter if you hunt with a bow, rifle or muzzleloader, a laser rangefinder will make you a better deer hunter above and beyond telling you how far away the target is.

In terms of technology, today's laser rangefinders are light years ahead of the units available even five years ago. Contemporary units are much more rugged, use far less battery power and can withstand more physical and environmental abuse.

As an example, I was recently speaking with an Army special forces sniper. He told me he and many of his contemporaries buy the same laser rangefinders you can buy for hunting and use them on their missions in Iraq and Afghanistan.

"After about a year of using one of them, I started having some problems with it," he said. "So I opened the unit up and dumped about a shot glass full of sand out of it. It was still working, though. It just started working a bit faster once the sand was gone."

That said, there is more to using a laser rangefinder than meets the eye. Here are some quick tips on how to get the most out of yours.

First, never buy a unit without an angle-compensating feature that helps tell you the distance to aim for, not the line-of-sight distance to the target.

All the top-end units today have this feature. If your old unit does not, it is worth spending the money and upgrading to a new unit that does.

Many units today also give you the ability to focus the eyepiece, something not possible several years ago. Even if your eyesight is 20-20, this is a valuable feature.

> IF YOU'RE A SERIOUS WHITETAIL HUNTER, YOU PROBABLY ALREADY OWN A LASER RANGEFINDER. IF YOU DO NOT, YOU NEED TO PUT ONE ON THE TOP OF YOUR WISH LIST.

EASY MODIFICATIONS

The first thing I do is pad my entire rangefinder with stick-on moleskin, then wrap the whole thing again with the same tape hockey players use to wrap their sticks.

Hockey tape is sort of like duct tape, but it remains flexible when temperatures go below freezing. This wrapping helps protect the unit. It also helps muffle any inadvertent clunks or clanks should you accidentally bump it on something hard, such as a release aid or tree stand railing.

When I'm bowhunting, I wear my rangefinder on a long cord looped over my neck and under my right armpit. It hangs about belt level, which means I can tuck it into a coat pocket. This makes it easy for me to quickly grab the rangefinder without looking at it, focus on an approaching deer, and let it drop out of the way while I hook up my release and turn an arrow loose.

It doesn't matter if you hunt with a bow, rifle or muzzle-loader, a laser rangefinder will make you a better deer hunter above and beyond telling you how far away the target is.

However you choose to wear it, put some thought into how you will use it. Make sure you have a way to easily access and put it away so you can shoot quickly.

This tip sounds simple, but it's often overlooked: Always have a spare battery. What good is a rangefinder if you can't use it?

One time I was changing my battery in a tree stand when I dropped the battery compartment cover to the ground. It was gone forever.

To keep my unit functioning, I placed a small wad of aluminum foil on top of the battery and held it in place with duct tape. When I got home, I called the company, and they sent me a new cover.

For spot-and-stalk hunting in open country, rangefinders perform another valuable function. It's not uncommon to see a buck you want to stalk and wonder, "How far do I have to go to get in range?"

First, take a reading off the buck. Then take a reading off a rock, bush, tree or the lip of a gully between you and the deer. Subtract that reading from the deer and you can choose your destination point.

DON'T MAKE IT A CRUTCH

Of course, don't become too reliant on a rangefinder. It is often not possible to use your rangefinder when a deer sneaks up on you.

That means you need to be able to "eyeball" the range. I use my rangefinder to train myself to do this.

One of my favorite drills is to "stump shoot" using a judo or bludgeon-type point. While walking around, I pick out a tuft of grass, leaf or some other soft target and shoot at it without using my rangefinder. After the shot, I take a range reading that tells me how close I was at guessing the exact range.

I do the same out of my tree stands, often shooting one practice arrow into the ground before getting down after a morning shift. ■

chapter 17

GET LOOPY FOR CONSISTENT ACCURACY

▶ BEING SOMETHING OF AN "ANTI-GADGETEER," I was pretty skeptical when string loops appeared on the hunting scene. Why tie something onto your bow-string that might slide around or come loose when all you had to do was clip the release aid's jaws to the string?

Then I began watching some top-notch tournament archers make the switch. It wasn't long before all of them — guys who cannot afford faulty equipment — were using string loops. Next, I shared bow-hunting camp with Pete Shepley, one of archery's most innovative and creative minds and the founder of PSE Archery. When he told me I should be shooting a loop, I took his advice to heart. I haven't gone without one since.

GETTING STARTED

A string loop — which is sometimes referred to as a release rope — is nothing more than a small loop of heavy-duty nylon string or cord permanently attached to the bow-string.

Instead of using a standard nock set, you tie the loop above and below the arrow nock, leaving just enough room between the bow-string and the loop to clip on the jaws of the release aid after the

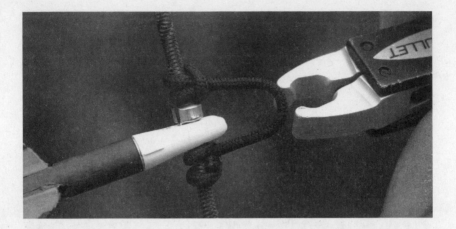

arrow has been nocked. Basically, the string loop acts as both the nock set and the connector between the release aid and bow-string.

A string loop — which is sometimes referred to as a release rope — is nothing more than a small loop of heavy-duty nylon string or cord permanently attached to the bow-string.

To tie a string loop, you need some heavy nylon cord, a bow square, pair of scissors or knife and a butane lighter. Personally, I buy nylon cord by the foot. It is much more affordable than buying pre-cut pieces of "string loop cord."

Before you can tie the loop, you need to use a bow square to find where the loop should go on the bow-string. Most people start with a nock point about ⅛-inch above center. Mark that point on the bow-string and keep the top knot of your string loop just above that mark as a reference.

Cut 6 inches of cord to make the loop. It is tied using a pair of reversed half-hitch knots. The reversed half-hitches pull against each other. If you need some guidance, your local pro shop professional can show you how to tie one in no time. Don't leave much of a loop, and don't snug the knots down tight. Also, make sure you have short tag ends extending an inch or so past the knots.

After loosely tying the top part of the loop onto the string, adjust it to the estimated proper nock height using the bow square. Then, place an arrow nock in the center of the loop, which will allow you to create the proper spacing. Insert a pair of needle-nose pliers into the loop and forcefully open them. This will stretch open the loop and tighten the half-hitch knots.

Play with the loop until it is short enough to leave only a smidgen of space between the arrow nock and release jaws. When you've got it right and everything tightened up, use a lighter to carefully burn the tag ends of the cord until the excess is gone and a hardened bulb is left at the ends. Don't burn the bow-string! This hardened tag end is enough to keep the knots from pulling through, although some shooters dab a little epoxy on "just in case."

When the loop is in place, proceed with bow tuning just as you would with a conventional nock set. At first, the string loop can probably be slid up and down for tuning. But after the pressure of several draws is placed on the knots, they will begin to grip even tighter. They will eventually become unmovable. However, being somewhat of a "doubting Thomas," I usually crimp a standard nock above the loop to prevent any slippage.

BECAUSE A STRING LOOP EXTENDS BEHIND THE BOW-STRING AT FULL DRAW, IT WILL ESSENTIALLY SHORTEN YOUR DRAW LENGTH BY THE LENGTH OF THE LOOP.

POSSIBLE PROBLEMS

Because a string loop extends behind the bow-string at full draw, it will essentially shorten your draw length by the length of the loop. That's the main reason loops should be tied as short as possible. To overcome this, take it into account when buying a bow. For example, I am a 28½-inch draw, but I buy bows with a 28-inch draw. Using a release with an adjustable wrist strap can help, too. Of course, if the loop is not tied tightly, it can creep slightly up the bow-string. Creeping will effect the bow's tune and your anchor point.

String loops can also be a bit slower to use, because most bow-hunters must move their eyes to their loop to get their release at-tached. Using a single-jaw release with a semi-open jaw designed specifically for string loops can help.

A MAJOR ADVANTAGE

Why, then, should you use a string loop?

"It relieves the unbalanced pressures on the arrow nock/string," Shepley explained on that hunt many years ago. It makes the shot quieter, prevents unnecessary bow-string serving wear, and if you use a release aid that does not attach itself to your wrist with a strap, you can attach the release to the loop and leave it there while sitting in your stand.

"I promise you that a loop will make you a more accurate bow shot," Shepley added.

The final verdict? If you have not made the switch to a string loop, perhaps it's time you did. ■

chapter 18

CHOOSING A RELEASE FOR STRING LOOPS

▶ MORE BOWHUNTERS ARE ADDING a string loop to their bow-strings than ever before. The reason is simple: The combination of a string loop and quality release aid creates the most accurate way to shoot an arrow.

Tying a loop is fairly simple. It's something you can either do yourself or have done at your local pro shop. However, beyond that, you must select a release aid to mate with your loop.

There are three basic release aid models that work well with a string loop — the dual-jaw caliper, single-jaw caliper and a single caliper designed expressly for a loop. Each has pluses and minuses.

The dual-jaw caliper release is the most popular design sold today. It is used by both string loop shooters and archers who attach the release directly to the bowstring. It has two movable jaws that open and close simultaneously. There are many different makes and models to choose from.

The single-jaw caliper release is also popular. This release features one movable jaw, and one stationary jaw. The theory is that with only one moving jaw, it is easier to get a consistent release than when using a release with two movable jaws.

Special string loop release aids are essentially single-jaw caliper releases. The difference between them and a standard single-jaw release is that instead of the two jaws coming together and touching when the release is closed around the string loop, there is a small open space after the release has been attached to the loop. The advantage is that the release can be attached or removed from the string loop without activating. With a little practice, it is easy to attach the release to the loop without looking at it — a feature that can be nice when you do not want to take your eyes off an approaching deer, even for a second or two.

Choosing which release make, model and style you use is an individual thing. All these styles get the job done. I

I have tried all three release aid styles, but seem to gravitate back to the traditional dual-jaw caliper because it works well for me. It is much more important to set the bow up properly, and this is where the pro shop can help you.

THE DUAL-JAW CALIPER RELEASE IS THE MOST POPULAR DESIGN SOLD TODAY. IT IS USED BY BOTH STRING LOOP SHOOTERS AND ARCHERS WHO ATTACH THE RELEASE DIRECTLY TO THE BOWSTRING.

If you simply tie a string loop onto the bow without giving any consideration to the type of release you'll be using, bad things can happen.

How so?

I see many shooters each year with a string loop that is too long. A string loop shortens your draw length because the release is not attached to the bowstring itself, but at a point slightly behind the string. This will knock up to ½-inch off your draw length. It doesn't seem like a lot, but it takes a bit off your power stroke, which will cost you some raw arrow speed.

Make sure your release aid's wrist strap is adjustable. Being able to lengthen or shorten the wrist strap will enable you to precisely establish the proper length, which will permit you to anchor properly.

If the loop is too large, you also risk not being able to anchor properly because you'll have to pull your shoulder, arm and hand farther behind your jaw or ear (or whatever anchor point you use). This can wreak havoc with your shooting form, which can adversely affect accuracy.

On the other hand, if the loop is tied too short, it is possible that your release aid jaws will not be able to be easily inserted into the loop itself.

If your release aid has a wrist strap — the vast majority do — you must make sure the strap is adjustable. Being able to lengthen or shorten the wrist strap will enable you to precisely establish the proper length, which will permit you to anchor properly.

It is also important that your release aid have an easily-adjustable trigger. There are two schools of thought on how the trigger is best activated. The first is to squeeze it like a rifle trigger. This is how I shoot. The second involves flexing your back muscles while your index finger is on the trigger, with the subsequent pressure setting the trigger off by surprise. Either way, you need to be able to adjust the trigger pull until it is at a comfortable pressure.

Most release aids come with their triggers set a bit stiff for my taste, so I take a little pressure off.

If you have not tried some of the latest release aids, I recommend you head down to your pro shop and check them out. Bring your bow so you can shoot them with your own string loop and see how the combination works for you.

Even if you do not choose to buy a new release, there is a good chance you will find that you need to adjust your release/string loop combination a until it more perfectly fits your body size and shooting style.

There is no downside in that. ∎

chapter 19

DO YOU NEED LIGHTED PINS?

▶ I BELIEVE IN SIMPLICITY and try and avoid any gimmickry when it comes to my equipment. After all, the more stuff you add, the more chance there is for something you've come to rely on to fail. So for years, I avoided using bow sights that have lights to illuminate the pins.

I had many reasons: For one, these sights are not legal in all states. For another, many of the lighting systems found on sights even five years ago were pretty cheesy. Plus, up until last season, I was doing a fair amount of filming, which meant I couldn't shoot unless there was enough camera light anyway.

Then, a couple seasons ago, a huge 8-point walked within five steps of my stand just as the morning light began to reveal his shape against the ground. He hung around my stand for several minutes. At one point, he was 20 yards off and I could see the outline of his antlers and his white throat patch. There was no way I could see my pins well enough to even think about shooting. Then and there, I decided to set up a bow with a lighted pin sight and experiment with it for hunting.

WHEN DO LIGHTED PINS WORK BEST?

Lighted pins don't help in every circumstance you might face, but they are nice in certain situations. I've found their best use is when hunting from a darkened ground blind or sitting in a tree stand where I am covered up among dark branches. It might be bright outside, but your pins become invisible in the shade without the additional light. Where legal, I always use lighted pins in a ground blind.

Most of today's fiber-optic sight pins are so efficient at soaking up ambient light they don't need the help of battery-powered, sight-mounted lights. Should you use one? It depends on your individual needs — and your state's regulations.

What about during the first and last few minutes of daylight? This is when I thought lighted pins would be most helpful. However, I have been surprised that this is not necessarily the case. Here's why: Today's fiber-optic sight pins are so good at soaking up light they don't need the help. Modern fibers allow me to make shots at reasonable distances in light that is very dim. And when it is so dark that the fiber optic pins are no longer bright enough to use alone, turning on the light means the deer's body will just become nothing more than a dark blob. To me, taking a shot under these conditions is unethical because you cannot pick a precise point to place the illuminated pin.

CHOOSING A LIGHT SOURCE

There are some add-on sight lights for archers who want to use their existing unlighted bow sights. I have tried several of these and, in every case, found I could never get them attached securely while shining directly onto the sight's top pin.

LIGHTED PINS DON'T HELP IN EVERY CIRCUMSTANCE YOU MIGHT FACE, BUT THEY ARE NICE IN CERTAIN SITUATIONS. I'VE FOUND THEIR BEST USE IS WHEN HUNTING FROM A DARKENED GROUND BLIND OR SITTING IN A TREE STAND WHERE I AM COVERED UP AMONG DARK BRANCHES.

Luckily, many companies now incorporate a light, or light bracket, onto their sights. Yet, because all our eyes see things differently, I would recommend checking out multiple sights with built-in lights before making a purchase.

For example, being closer to 60 than 50, my eyes are not quite what they used to be. That means when I extend my bow to shoot, my sight pins get just a tad fuzzy. Because of this, when I use pins .029-inch and larger and hit them with a light, they glow enough that they sort of "blob out." Precisely placing them on a deer's chest becomes difficult when this happens. I use smaller-diameter, .019-inch pins instead. It makes a difference.

Will lighted pins help? It's an individual call. I use them at times, but I never rely on them totally. My advice: Try them out and decide for yourself. ■

chapter 20

EXAMINING MODERN SPLIT-LIMB BOWS

▶ I REMEMBER WHEN the first split-limb bows appeared back in the 1980s — before the technology was refined. Archers weren't impressed, and the design fell away for a decade. Today, split-limb bows are back in a big way. Still, questions remain: Why do we need split-limb bows? And, are they as strong, reliable and accurate as solid-limb bows?

HISTORICAL PERSPECTIVE

In the old days, solid-limb designs sometimes cracked after repeated flexing. This problem was a result of how they were made.

Generally, limbs are fabricated of a laminated material which is stronger along the length of the limb than across it. For greatest flexing strength, the limb is made up of incremental strips which run the length of the limb from its point of attachment at the riser to the end receiving the pulley axle. Adjacent strips are typically held together with adhesives, and the limb is covered by a reinforcing laminate.

The strips at the outer edges of the limb run the entire length of the limb and directly receive the flexing stress when the bow is drawn. However, strips located in the middle of the limb terminate somewhere along the limb crotch. These interior strips do not directly receive the flexing force and have a tendency to resist flexing as the bow is drawn. Only the interstrip cohesive forces transfer stress to the interior strips from the outer strips. Since the interfiber cohesive forces are not as strong as the strips themselves, the interior strips do not receive as much longitudinal stress as the outer strips. As a result, the limb has a tendency to develop significant transverse tensional stresses, which concentrate at the area where the crotch is deepest. After repeated flexing, the concentrated transverse tensional stresses eventually tend to overcome the cohesive forces and cause separation of adjacent strips. A crack can develop near the end of the crotch.

TODAY, SPLIT-LIMB BOWS ARE BACK IN A BIG WAY. STILL, QUESTIONS REMAIN: WHY DO WE NEED SPLIT-LIMB BOWS? AND, ARE THEY AS STRONG, RELIABLE AND ACCURATE AS SOLID-LIMB BOWS?

Another problem experienced by conventional compound bows is the torsional stress exerted on the bow limb by the pulleys. The stress can cause the bow limbs to be pulled out of vertical alignment with the riser and each other. If the bow limbs are not properly aligned, the bow will not shoot straight.

Prior methods for preventing the limb from splitting included applying a reinforcing patch near the bottom of the crotch, installing a bolt or rivet beneath the crotch, and using a harness yoke for the dead-end connection of the bus cables attached to the bow pulleys to achieve uniform stress distribution across the limb. However, none of these methods completely eliminates the potential cracking of bow limbs. In addition, the use of reinforcing bolts or patches increases the weight of the bow limb and reduces the bow limb acceleration.

INCEPTION OF THE SPLIT

The first patent for a split-limb compound bow (Caldwell U.S. Pat. No. 4,350,138) was issued to Joseph M. Caldwell in 1980 and disclosed a

Much like today's solid-limb compound bows, modern split-limb bows are extremely tough, durable, fast and accurate.

forked bow limb that was split axially for a substantial portion of the length of the limb. The split divided the limb into two portions held together by means such as a bracket at a point inboard of the crotch. When the bow is drawn, the limb portions flex together essentially as though the limb were unsplit along its length. The bracket, however, interferes with the flexing of the limb along its entire length. Also, the bow limb members are not separate and independent and thus remain subject to splitting. As time went on other innovators continued to explore the potential of split limbs, and on March 3, 1998, patent number 5,722,380 was issued to Spencer Land and Clint Pierce of High Country Archery. These designs became the basis of modern split-limb technology.

SPLIT FOR STRENGTH

Fast forward to today. Controlled stress tests on bow limbs show that some solid limbs can begin to fail after about 25 dry fires. Most often, they start to crack where the V-groove is where the cam is mounted. Cracks sometimes also occur where the limb mounts to the riser.

For comparison, Hoyt (a company that offers an array of split-limb compound bows) has engineered a patented ¾-inch Split Limb Technology to survive an amazing 1,000 dry fires at 80 pounds draw weight and 30-inch draw length. The design also eliminates the V-groove and limb bolt groove or hole where failure most often occurs on traditional solid limbs.

Does all this mean that solid limb bows are on their way to the scrap heap?

Of course not. Modern solid-limb compounds are more reliable, fast and accurate than ever before. What it does show is that modern split-limb bows are extremely tough, durable, fast and accurate, too. ■

chapter 21

SHOULD YOU SHOOT A SHORTER VANE?

▶ ARCHERS ARE ALWAYS LOOKING FOR A WAY to make their arrows fly faster and more accurately. When the cedar shafts shot by Doug Easton in the 1940s and 1950s proved more inconsistent than he wanted, he gave us aluminum shafts. Then, as compound bows improved, aluminum shafts changed to meet the performance potential of better bows. Aluminum shafts were then challenged by a carbon. Although carbon shafts had some initial problems with straightness and durability, it wasn't long before they became the dominant option.

As arrow shafts evolved, they became lighter and smaller in diameter. Broadhead manufacturers also began using modern materials, replacing heavy steel ferrules with aircraft-grade aluminum. Inserts that allowed broadheads to be easily screwed into the end of the arrow rather than glued on also saved weight.

At the other end of the shaft, fletching has also become smaller and lighter.

Today, the most popular vane size used by bowhunters who shoot state-of-the-art compound bows and carbon arrows is the 2-inch long vane.

According to Brady Arview of New Archery Products, tournament archers have gone even smaller, often using 1½-inch long vanes.

"Ten to 15 years ago, when fatter, heavier aluminum shafts tipped with 125-grain broadheads were the standard and bows launched them at an average of less than 250 feet per second, it took larger 5-inch vanes to stabilize the shaft in flight," Arview said.

However, as bows became more efficient, arrow shafts became

High Speed Lessons

Just how many revolutions does a broadhead-tipped arrow shaft complete before striking a target 30 yards downrange when shot from a popular modern compound bow with an initial velocity of 260 fps?

The answer: Zero.

Yep, you read that right.

Most folks believe that an arrow in flight rotates rapidly as it sails downrange. However, high-speed photography shows that a carbon shaft straight-fletched with standard 2-inch plastic vanes does not even rotate one time at 30 yards from a bow shooting about 260 fps. If you add a bit of offset — say 2 degrees — you will get the shaft to rotate perhaps two or three revolutions at 30 yards. That's it.

However, NAP's 2-inch QuikSpin vanes fletched either straight or with a small offset, produce a shaft that will rotate at least 10 times at 30 yards. And there's no doubt that the more a projectile (be it bullet, football or arrow shaft) rotates while in flight, the more consistently accurate it will be.

Here's another old wife's tale: Years ago, it was common to read that you should try to line up your fletches with your broadhead blades for maximum accuracy.

Again, the high speed photography disproves this claim. The photography shows it makes no difference whatsoever in accuracy.

What is important is making sure your broadheads are screwed in perfectly straight to the shaft. You can check that with the spin test — spinning the arrow on the broadhead tip – to see if there is any wobble.

lighter, and 100-grain heads became the most popular option, smaller fletches were required to stabilize the shaft.

"The 4-inch vane became the most popular," Arview said. "Then it was the 3- or 3½-inch size. Today it's the 2-inch fletch."

Simply stated, smaller vanes match the smaller diameter of the most popular carbon shaft and lighter, low-profile broadheads, which helps balance the entire arrow. The result is more accuracy.

Not only have vanes become shorter, they have also become a bit taller and more rigid than the plastic vanes of old.

NAP's Quikfletch and QuikSpin vanes are about a half-inch taller than the old 4-inch vanes. This added height and stiffness is plenty to stabilize the small-diameter broadhead-tipped shafts most modern bowhunters use.

The new vanes are also quieter. Older vanes were made of a more flexible material. They flexed more in flight, which caused more noise, more drag and less speed than modern vanes.

Simply stated, smaller vanes match the smaller diameter of the most popular carbon shaft and lighter, low-profile broadheads, which helps balance the entire arrow. The result is more accuracy.

So, is there such a thing as fletches that are too large for modern arrows?

Arview doesn't think so.

"Within reason, they will certainly adequately stabilize modern arrow shafts," he said. "The question, though, is why would you use something that weighs more than you need it to or provides more drag and, thus, less raw arrow speed?"

Still, he believes most archers would benefit from the new designs.

What's right for you and your bowhunting rig? The answer can be found with a trip to your archery pro shop.

If you are shooting the same longer fletches you used five years ago, try some new shafts fletched with smaller vanes. See if making this small change will tune well in your bow, give you more arrow speed and tighten up your broadhead groups. Then you can decide whether making a change is worth while. ■

chapter 22

SILENCE IS GOLDEN... AND CHEAP

▶ IT'S A SIMPLE, UNDENIABLE FACT: Even when a hunter is using one of the high-tech bows manufactured today, a whitetail has the ability to hear and react to a shot before the arrow smacks it in the ribs. That's because sound travels at approximately 1,129 feet per second. Even if you shoot an arrow at 300 fps, the sound of the bow going off will reach a deer's ears almost four times faster than the shaft. Thus, an alert and incredibly agile whitetail has time to "jump the string."

Fortunately, bow manufacturers are now producing bows and matching accessories that remove a lot of the vibration and noise from their products. A slug of aftermarket products are also available to help make your bow quieter.

If a bow is unusually noisy, vibrations from one or more accessories added onto the bow itself are usually the cause. Here's how you can quickly check and easily repair problems that might cost you a deer without a big financial hit.

DIAGNOSING THE PROBLEM

If you hear noise at the shot and are not sure exactly where it is coming from, be methodical trying to find it. First, try plucking the

bowstring just an inch or so. Listen for vibrating parts. A partner will be a big help.

If the source isn't obvious, I always suspect a bow quiver. However, it might be necessary to take each accessory off one at a time and repeat the string-plucking process until the source of the noise has been isolated.

Use fleece or moleskin on any exposed surface that can make contact with the arrow, including the prongs or launcher arms and the bottom of the bow sight.

ABSORB THE SHOCK

If your string twangs like a badly-tuned guitar, you have a number of options. Manufacturers produce many "string silencers," all designed to be placed on the string approximately 6 inches from each axle. They are made of several different materials, including fleece, soft rubber, or LimbSaver's unique NAVCOM material. Their purpose is to absorb some of the noise-causing vibration associated with the string coming to an abrupt halt. Most string silencers can be easily attached to the bowstring without the need of a bow press. Similar products are designed for the cable system. However, it's also important to check the cable bar and cable slide for smoothness.

Vibration absorbers are also used to control limb vibration, which can be the source of a lot of noise. Most have an adhesive backing and are easy to apply. Others fit between split limbs. All of these are inexpensive items and will not affect a bow's accuracy. A stabilizer can also absorb a lot of vibration. I like stabilizers that are gel or hydro filled. The bonus is these items also aid in accuracy.

> **IF A BOW IS UNUSUALLY NOISY, VIBRATIONS FROM ONE OR MORE ACCESSORIES ADDED ONTO THE BOW ITSELF ARE USUALLY THE CAUSE.**

THE REST OF THE STORY

The first thing I do when I set up a bow is nock an arrow, put it on the rest and then deliberately move the arrow around and off the rest to see exactly where it will contact the bow if it were to accidentally fall off. If it can, it will definitely make a wicked clanging sound. The solution? Put some fleece or moleskin on any exposed surface that can make contact with the arrow, including the prongs or launcher arms and the bottom of the bow sight.

Speaking of bow sights, movable parts on a sight are often the source of squeaking and groaning. It's often a function of screws vibrating loose. I use light machine oil to lubricate the screw threads, and then I constantly check them for looseness.

DON'T QUIVER

The easiest way to eliminate noise is to use a removable quiver. If you prefer to keep the quiver attached, you should know the problems it can cause and take preventative steps.

First, make sure the foam insert in the quiver hood is in tight, with no air pockets. Also, make sure the foam holds the broadheads snuggly and the arrow grippers hold the shafts tightly to eliminate vibration. If the grip is loose, make the fit tighter by adding a layer of either tape or moleskin to the grippers.

Eliminate any potential contact between the quiver and any part of the bow during a shot. If you find areas of contact, cover them with fleece or moleskin. If you still hear vibrations, try sticking a small vibration absorber to the hood.

One other note on bow quivers: Instead of carrying six or eight arrows in my quiver, I only carry four or five. I space the arrows apart so the fletches do not touch (and vibrate).

MOVING PARTS

Lubricating moving parts is important both for a bow's mechanical life and the reduction of friction noise. This includes axles, but I also lubricate limb bolts and any other screw threads on both the bow and its accessories.

In hot weather, a quality penetrating oil like WD-40 or RemOil works great. But when temperatures start to drop, I switch over to products designed to work in sub-zero weather. ■

chapter 23

SET YOUR SIGHTS ON SIMPLICITY

▶ IN THE PAST DECADE, compound bow accessories have come a very long way. From arrow rests, to bow quivers, to vibration dampening add-ons, these accessories — when chosen with care to compliment both the bow and your shooting style — all help make you a more efficient shooter.

Yet, few accessories have evolved like the bow sight.

I vividly remember the earliest multiple-pin sights I used back in the late 1970s and early 1980s. Compared to the sights available today they were awful. But back then, they were cutting edge.

Most simply bolted into the riser, and unless you added a lot of moleskin between the riser and sight bracket, they rattled like an earthquake. The pins were nothing more than brass rods with a roundish tip that slid into a bracket with two adjacent vertical slots so the pins could be slid up and down for elevation changes. The pins were held in place by a square metal washer and awkward thumbscrew.

Windage adjustments were made by sliding the entire bracket east and west. Nothing moved smoothly, and everything rattled loose, meaning you had to check everything daily.

The pin guard was a square metal bracket that couldn't keep a kid out of a cookie jar. And if you had to take a shot on the cusp of daylight, the pins disappeared faster than a politician backpedaling on a campaign promise.

Twenty years later, top-end hunting bow sights are precision tools manufactured with tight tolerances, easy adjustment capabilities, and sight pins even my tired old eyes can see in dim light. They are micro-adjustable, easy and quick to install, and can take a beating in the deer woods and still hold their zero.

If you have not checked out new bow sights in the past five years, you owe it to yourself to do so. When you do, remember there are a lot of choices out there, and the only person you need to please is yourself. Look at several different makes, models and styles, and ask if you can shoot a bow with the models you are considering before you buy.

A top-quality bow sight is going to set you back somewhere between $75 and $150, but it's a purchase you will never regret making and a product that will last for decades.

Here are some considerations:

HOW MANY PINS?

Many whitetail hunters want as few pins as possible to avoid confusion at crunch time. Some of my friends use just three pins, but most have five, set in 10 yard increments between 20 and 60 yards. To take advantage of the speed and accuracy of modern compounds, you should learn to shoot out to at least 40 yards.

Don't use my sight as an example. Since I shoot the same bow for everything, from tree stand whitetails to western big game, I have nine pins on my sights, set at 10 yard increments.

MOVABLE OR FIXED?

Some bowhunters like a single-pin sight with a movable bracket.

This type of sight is designed to allow the archer to move the single pin to correspond with marks on the bracket that will place the pin in the right spot for various distances. Then, when the time comes the hunter moves the sight and holds dead-on for the shot. Most archers find this too complicated. Me, too.

PIN GUARDS

Few bow sight innovations are more conducive to accurate shooting than a round pin guard that can be precisely aligned with a round peep sight hole.

This allows just one more check at full draw that your head is in the proper position and your sight pin centered in the peep's hole. If the pin guard has a bright outline, so much the better.

A small bubble level helps archers ensure that the sight has been installed perfectly level on the bow — an often-overlooked detail. It also offers a quick reference when you come to full draw to help you avoid canting the bow.

LOW-LIGHT SHOOTING

Some fiber optic pins are brighter than others. For example models that wrap a long fiber around a circular drum can really pick up a lot of light.

There are two keys to fiber optic pins. The first is that the fragile fiber optic material itself must be protected in some manner, or it will eventually break.

Second, the pins must use a color your eyes can see well in dim light. My eyes see green pins extremely well and red pins very poorly, so I try and use as many green pins on my sight as possible.

I also look for a sight that makes changing sight pins quick and easy.

EASY, PRECISE ADJUSTMENTS

When shopping for a new sight also keep in mind that you will eventually have to adjust the pins. You should be able to quickly and easily adjust your sight pins up and down, and be able to easily adjust the entire rack of pins both left and right and up and down.

If it takes a rocket scientist to make these adjustments, keep shopping.

DO YOU NEED A BUBBLE?

Many sights come with a small bubble level installed at the base of the pin guard. This is a wonderful addition for two reasons.

First, it helps you ensure that the sight has been installed on the bow perfectly level — a very important, yet often-overlooked part of installing the sight. A sight that is not level encourages your arrows to hit left or right of center as you move down the rack of pins.

And second, the level is a quick reference when you come to full draw that keeps you from canting the bow — which also can cause left and right misses.

SIMPLE OPERATION

Finally, in all things archery, the acronym KISS – Keep It Simple, Stupid – certainly applies to bow sights.

I like bow sights that require a minimum of Allen wrench sizes to make all the adjustments. Also, the fewer moving parts that can rattle loose the better.

Parts that do move should be able to be tightly secured.

Remember, the whole purpose of a bow sight is to allow you to acquire the target as quickly as possible, then place your broadhead into the vitals shot after shot.

Buy a new sight that you are comfortable with, that will not break under even rugged field use and is reliable as the sunrise.

This is one accessory in which I believe the upgrade is well worth the money. ∎

chapter 24

WHY BRACE HEIGHT MATTERS

▶ THE LAST THING YOU NEED to think about when a whitetail walks within bow range is some technical mumbo-jumbo about how your compound bow functions. Judgments about your setup should be taken care of well before the season begins so that all you need to do is concentrate on not being seen, smelled or heard. Then all you need to do is smoothly draw the bow back, place the proper pin on the deer's vitals and turn the arrow loose.

That's why, when it is time to trade in your vintage compound bow for a new, improved version, you first need to understand a bit about the features and benefits of the various bow designs available that year so that you are comparing apples to apples.

One of the terms we often hear bandied about, yet most archers do not understand, is the term "brace height." What does it mean, exactly, and why should you be concerned about it?

Brace height certainly isn't as sexy as AMO or IBO arrow speeds, the mass weight of the bow, or its axle-to-axle length. Yet brace height is something every deer hunter should understand.

The Archery Trade Association defines brace height as the perpendicular distance from the bowstring to the pivot point of the bow's handle. That pivot point is the most recessed part of the bow

handle and is usually located directly below the hole drilled for the arrow rest. Brace height is measured in inches, and the brace height of your bow definitely affects both its speed and accuracy potential. Here's why.

The brace height of a compound bow is defined as the dimension from the grip pivot point to the inside edge of the bow string measured at 90 degrees with the bow in the undrawn condition.

The shorter the brace height, the farther the bowstring travels forward upon release. This creates a longer power stroke, which, in turn, increases raw arrow speed (all other things being equal). Today's fastest compound bows have brace heights as short as 5½ inches. Meanwhile, some models have brace heights as long as 8 inches.

If short brace heights produce more speed, why choose a bow with a longer brace height? That's simple: accuracy.

Bows with brace heights of less than 6½ inches can be very critical of shooting form and are less forgiving because of the extreme angles created by the string and limbs at full draw (this can be compounded in bows with a shorter overall axle-to-axle length) and because the arrow stays on the string longer. This makes your shooting form, and especially hand torque, much more important to accurate arrow flight.

Bows with short brace heights are also more prone to slap your bow arm with the string, especially when you are wearing heavy clothing.

Conversely, bows with longer brace heights are a bit slower but are much easier to shoot accurately. That's because the power stroke is shorter, and the arrow is not on the bowstring as long. Thus, minor shooting form errors — while still troublesome — are not quite as critical to placing the arrow on target.

Of course, a bow's brace height is just one of many design features that affect how fast the bow shoots and how "shootable" it is. However, it is one of the features you should consider when shopping for a new bow.

My own rule of thumb on brace height is this: For the average whitetail hunter faced with what most of us would consider common, everyday hunting conditions, a compound bow with a brace height between 7 and 8 inches is a solid compromise between "shootability" and raw arrow speed.

FOR THE AVERAGE WHITETAIL HUNTER, A COMPOUND BOW WITH A BRACE HEIGHT BETWEEN 7 AND 8 INCHES IS A SOLID COMPROMISE BETWEEN "SHOOTABILITY" AND RAW ARROW SPEED.

Keep in mind that with the advances in modern compound bow design, the bows we have to choose from today are so much faster than ever before, it is no longer necessary to shoot a bow with a super-short brace height to achieve raw arrow speeds that only the most radical of bow designs could produce just a decade ago. Therefore, most compound bows with brace heights of between 7 and 8 inches will send hunting weight arrows downrange at speeds somewhere between 250 and 280 fps — plenty fast to get the job done.

These same bows, when properly tuned and sighted in, will be comfortable to shoot and extremely accurate. They'll also allow you to shoot well even when your body is contorted, the weather's nasty, and the deer do not do exactly what you had hoped they would — pretty much standard fare when bowhunting whitetails. ■

chapter 25

THE PRACTICAL, LITTLE BOW PEEP

▶ IF YOU SHOOT A COMPOUND BOW without using a peep sight, chances are pretty good that you are not the best bow shot you can be.

A peep sight is nothing more than a small ring fitted into the bowstring above the nock point and positioned to align with your dominant eye at full draw. However, this little addition forces you to keep your head erect and anchor in a consistent spot shot after shot — important details in the quest to keep the same sight picture for every shot.

The knock on peep sights has been that they block too much of the available light at the cusp of dawn and dark from reaching your pupil, making it impossible to see your sight pins through the peep when light is this low. However, I find that by using a good fiber optic pin and large aperture peep, I can see my pins well enough to make shooting at game practical.

Some archers also worry that the peep won't be turned perfectly when they draw the bowstring, making it impossible to see through the aperture. However, this is rarely a problem if the peep is served correctly into the bowstring, and many models use a piece of surgical rubber tubing that pulls the peep into alignment each and every shot.

There are other downsides to peep sights, though they rarely occur. For example, a peep can fill with water during rainy weather, distorting your vision. I've even had a water droplet freeze inside the aperture hole, obliterating my vision. However, this is quickly remedied by sucking on the peep and letting your hot breath thaw it out.

When peeps first became popular with bow hunters, most models featured surgical rubber tubing to make sure they rotated into position at full draw. The tubing is cut so its length stretches it taut at full draw. This style was more popular a decade ago when bowstrings stretched much more than they do now, most bow hunters released their arrows using their fingers, and few release shooters had ever heard of a string loop.

A PEEP SIGHT IS NOTHING MORE THAN A SMALL RING FITTED INTO THE BOWSTRING ABOVE THE NOCK POINT AND POSITIONED TO ALIGN WITH YOUR DOMINANT EYE AT FULL DRAW.

But there are downsides to the tubing-dependent peep. First, the tubing can snag on brush or limbs and get pulled off the peep. The tubing will also crack and split over time and needs to be replaced. I've also had the knot that affixes the tubing to my bow come untied. Arrow speed is also affected. On average — and this varies from bow to bow — you'll lose about 5 fps of raw arrow speed using the tubing. Finally, when the bow is released, the tubing will fly forward and make a noticeable slapping sound that can help spook game.

Today, many archers use a style of peep that is called a self-centering peep. These jewels are designed to rotate into alignment without the aid of rubber tubing. They seem to be most consistently able to do this on modern bows featuring low- or non-stretch bowstrings

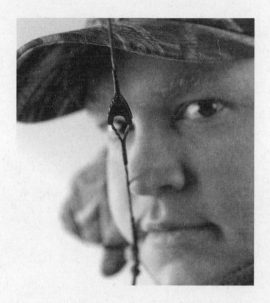

Peep sights come with different aperture sizes. For most whitetail hunting, larger apertures – which allow more light to pass through – are the best choice.

and a string loop. This combination allow the string to be drawn as consistently as possible, allowing the peep to rotate into position shot after shot.

Before serving a peep into its final position, you should shoot a couple hundred arrows with that string to get every little bit of stretch out of it. Then, the peep must be served securely into the string so it can't slip up and down between the strands. It is also important that your string loop be securely tied onto the bowstring so it will not rotate.

Peep placement can be crucial to accuracy. Make sure your peep is served into the bowstring so that your head can remain erect at full draw. After this position has been determined and the peep placed, mark the bowstring at the top and bottom of the peep with a white or silver marker. This will allow you to instantly tell if your peep has crept up or down the string (the usual direction is up).

I also shoot a lot of practice arrows aiming above or to the side of my peep with my top pin just in case something happens to my peep. I place the sight pin right on top on the peep, or in the middle off to the side. This practice lets me know where my arrows will strike at 20 yards in case the aperture gets filled with something, the peep doesn't rotate properly or the surgical tubing snaps or comes loose.

Several new peep variations deviate from the standard round hole, but they work in the same way. In most cases, the unique shape is meant to increase light transmission. Examples include the C-Peep, with an open slot along one side; the Vital Gear Master Peep, which clamps on the bowstring; and the String Splitter, which is more of an upside down "U" served into the bowstring with an open bottom that allows a huge amount of light in and increases your field of vision. ∎

chapter 26

YOU CAN BUILD A BETTER ARROW

▶ IF YOU'VE BEEN BOW HUNTING for any length of time, you've undoubtedly experienced the frustration of having a fletch tear, loosen, or get ripped right off one of your favorite hunting arrows.

Most hunters do one of two things — set the shaft aside for the rest of the season, or try to put the bad fletch back together again. The truth is, replacing a bad fletch on a carbon hunting shaft — the shaft of choice for the majority of today's bow hunters — isn't all that difficult. You just need a few simple tools, the right adhesive and a little time. And after you figure it out, the next step is to begin fletching all your own hunting shafts — something that takes a bit of time but results in precisely-built arrows that fly like rocket ships.

To get started you'll need to make a small investment in tools. First, you'll need a simple fletching jig. There are several good ones, including the Bohning Jig, Blitzenburger Dial-O-Fletch, Jo-Jan Multi-Fletcher, and Arizona Rim Products' Carbon E-Z Fletch, E-Z Fletch Pro and Fletch III.

Expect to spend somewhere between $50 and $100 for a quality fletcher. Next, you'll need a stripping tool for removing old fletches. A dull knife will work, but using one risks damaging the shaft. The Norway Zip-Strip works great and costs about $35. Cabela's sells a

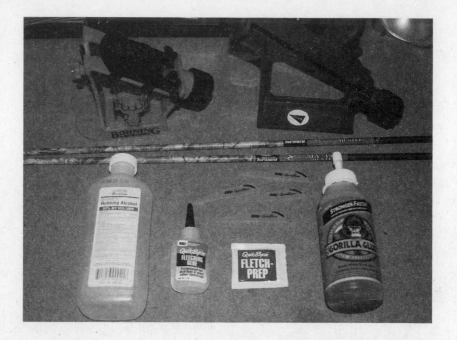

Fletch Stripper for $10.99 that also works well.

You'll need something to clean the shaft after the old fletches have been removed and to prep a new shaft for fletching. Acetone, lacquer thinner and denatured alcohol are some of the solutions that work well. Commercial products like New Archery Products' Quick Spin Fletch Prep Wipes, Bohning SSR Surface Cleaner and AAE Arrow Cleaner also do the job.

Finally, you'll need the proper adhesive to bond fletches to the shaft. Many years ago, Fletch-Tite was the standard by which fletching adhesives were judged. And it still works well — on aluminum shafts. Carbon shafts are best served by adhesives with a different chemical make-up — essentially, super glue-like adhesives. And these glues also work on aluminum arrows.

Top quality adhesives for carbon shafts include Carbon Express's CX ExpressBond, Bohning Fletch-Tite Platinum, Fast Fletch Glue, and Saunders Archery NPV Cement, among others. Commercial adhesives like Gorilla Glue and one of the many super glues like Locktite Professional also work. One product that has drawn raves from many folks is Goat Tuff Glue.

You'll also need a clean, level table to work on, some clean wiping clothes or paper towels, and a couple other little things described below, and then you're ready to get started.

Step One is to remove the damaged fletch. Do not think you can repair a small tear in a single fletch or properly re-glue a fletch to the shaft that is partially coming off and do the job right. Also, if you use "wraps" or some sort of shrink tube fletch system, you'll have to remove the entire thing and start over.

The most important part of adhesion is proper cleaning of the arrow shaft. Failure to do so can cause serious adhesion problems. After the old fletch has been removed, clean the shaft with a kitchen scrub pad and a commercial cleaner like Comet or Ajax, or one of the commercial shaft cleaners. Carefully wash all residue off, then rub the shaft with denatured alcohol to remove any fine particulates.

THE TRUTH IS, REPLACING A BAD FLETCH ON A CARBON HUNTING SHAFT ISN'T ALL THAT DIFFICULT. YOU JUST NEED A FEW SIMPLE TOOLS, THE RIGHT ADHESIVE, AND A LITTLE TIME.

Only scruff up the portion of the shaft to which fletches will be attached. You'll know when you are done when there is no more black coming off on your towel. Rinse the shaft in running hot water and let it air dry.

Arrows should be fletched as soon as possible after cleaning to keep the shaft from becoming contaminated. Do not touch the portion of the shaft to be fletched, or the base of the vane, or allow them to come into contact with any surface after they have been cleaned.

To fletch a shaft, place the arrow shaft in the jig. Next, place the vane in the clamp and apply an even bead of glue to the vane base. Don't use too much! Quickly apply the clamp to the magnet on the jig and press the fletch firmly to the shaft. Ensure the vane is in contact with the shaft, then let it stand for about five minutes.

Squeeze the clamp open and remove it from the vane. If you have more fletches to do, rotate the jig to the next position and apply the remaining vanes in the same manner. Remove the clamp after you have fletched your final vane.

Remove the arrow from the jig and dot both ends of each vane with adhesive. This will give you more vane support. ■

chapter 27

THE REST
IS UP TO YOU

▶ IN ALL FORMS OF SHOOTING, consistent accuracy is built upon a foundation that includes proper shooting mechanics, concentration and using a weapon-and-projectile combination that, when the shooter does his or her job, groups several shots closely together.

With a compound bow, it means tuning the bow-and-arrow combination until the arrows are flying like laser beams, with no wobble. Serious bowhunters paper-tune their bows until a broadhead-tipped shaft tears a bullet hole through the paper, a process that can be time-consuming but will pay huge dividends when it is time to make meat.

That's in a perfect world. In the real world, many bowhunters find the paper-tuning process nothing but drudgery.

Generally, one of two things happens. The first includes minor flaws in shooting form, often centered around hand torque. Gripping the bow improperly can cause the shooter to torque the handle as the shaft is released, which can cause minor inconsistencies in arrow flight. The second is more difficult to detect and may involve minor fletch contact with the arrow rest. Any contact with the rest will result in wobbly, inconsistent shaft flight that is magnified when broadhead blades, which like to steer the shaft just as fletching does, are added to the equation.

That's not to say that you cannot achieve superb arrow flight with broadheads using conventional arrow rests and smaller fletching. However, when you add the difficulties encountered in the field — weird body positions, awkward shooting angles, too many clothes in the way and a large dose of "buck fever" — the chances are good that the arrow will not fly exactly as it is supposed to. That's bad news.

With conventional arrow rests, archers depend on the position of the fletching to clear an arrow rest's prongs or launcher arms. The obvious answer has always been an arrow rest that supports the shaft prior to release, but then gets out of the way of the shaft once the string is released and the arrow starts forward.

FALL-AWAY ARROW RESTS PERMIT YOU TO ACCURATELY SHOOT FLETCHING LARGE ENOUGH TO STEER REPLACEABLE- AND FIXED-BLADE BROADHEADS. THEY ALSO HELP OVERCOME MINOR INCONSISTENCIES IN SHOOTING FORM, THE BANE OF MOST BOW-HUNTERS.

Enter the fall-away (also called "drop-away") arrow rest.

This radical concept is really pretty simple. Instead of using a conventional fixed-prong position to hold an arrow shaft at what is essentially a 90-degree angle to the bowstring, with a fall-away rest the shaft is laid on the riser shelf. The rest does have an arrow-holding launcher, but it is positioned below the shaft so it does not initially hold the shaft in place. In most cases, the launcher is connected to the bow's cable system — usually the down bus cable — either with a rubber tube, cord or cable. When the bow is drawn,

the rearward cable movement pulls the cord back, which in turn sends the launcher upward into the shaft, lifting it into position at full draw. When the string is released, the forward movement of the cable causes the launcher to rapidly "fall away" from the shaft. In essence, the arrow streaks forward with no chance of making further contact with the rest. The problem of fletch clearance has been solved.

When it was introduced a few years ago, the Zero Effect rest took accuracy to new levels, and sparked a revolution in the arrow-rest industry.

The concept sounds simple, and it is. But does it really work?

The fall-away rest concept came to the forefront in 2001, when Muzzy Products — best known for excellent lines of replaceable-blade broadheads — introduced their Zero Effect fall-away rest. As word of its success spread throughout the bowhunting community, other manufacturers could sense something of a revolution occurring. Since that time, a dazzling array of fall-away rests have been produced.

I am a firm believer in the old adage, "The proof is in the pudding." It took me a full season of hard-core experimenting before I was willing to admit that, guess what? Here is a new concept that really works and actually helps make most bowhunters better shooters. Since 2002, I have tested as many drop-aways as I could get my hands on, and I have bowhunted exclusively with them ever since.

I believe that fall-away arrow rests are the real deal. They permit you to accurately shoot fletching large enough to steer replaceable- and fixed-blade broadheads. They also help overcome minor inconsistencies in shooting form, the bane of most bowhunters. For thousands of bowhunters — myself included — the result has been more accurate broadhead shooting.

The key is to find one that works well with your make and model of compound bow and matches your style of hunting. The best place to check them out is at your local archery pro shop, where the expert shop help can explain the ins and outs and help you set your bow up with one the right way. If you've never put a drop-away rest on a bow, it can be a bit confusing and it is well worth the time and money to have an expert do it for you. ■

chapter 28

IT'S ALL ABOUT THE STRING

▶ A BOWSTRING HAS TWO MAIN PURPOSES — to transfer energy from your arms and back muscles to the limbs of the bow, and transfer that stored energy from the bow to the arrow. Just like a golf club or tennis racket, this created thrust propels the projectile (golf ball, tennis ball or arrow) and gives it direction. It must transfer energy efficiently, in a consistent manner, for many hundreds of shots. If the string doesn't meet these criteria, it's going to make it virtually impossible to shoot accurately with any consistency.

Modern bowstrings easily meet these basic criteria. However, all serious bowhunters should understand a few simple things about the string and how to maintain it.

There are two bowstring terms that are frequently misused and incorrectly interchanged. The first is "stretch." The proper and accurate definition of stretch is, "the temporary or recoverable elongation of the string caused by the shooting force of the bow." This is similar to what happens to your arm during the pulling on a rubber band — pull it and it stretches, let it go and it returns to its original shape.

"Creep" is the continual and permanent elongation of the bowstring caused by the load or tension from the limbs. This is akin to being hooked up to a torture rack and your arms and legs being

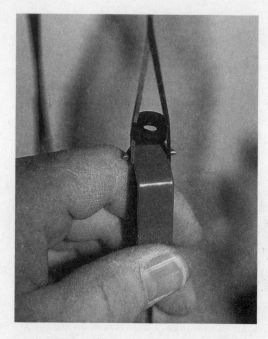

When installing peep sights, take the pressure off the string first with a commercial bow press. It's also important to take your time, being extra careful not to damage any of the string's fibers.

pulled in opposite directions for months.

One important thing to remember is that with many popular bowstring materials, it takes about 200 shots for the material to creep into the manufacturers' specified length. That's why with the strings found on many new bows it is important to shoot at least 200 times before doing your final fine-tuning and sighting in and serving in your peep sight.

Many top bow makers offer their bows with excellent bowstrings. However, as is the case with all things in life, not all bowstrings are created equal. Adding a custom string can add approximately $35 to $75 to a new bow purchase. However, many serious bowhunters feel they are worth it.

Many top tournament archers and bowhunters now use custom-made strings. The best ones I've found are found on bows built by BowTech, Mathews and custom strings by Winner's Choice Bow-strings.

Nearly all BowTech and Diamond bows include custom bowstrings. In fact, the company employs 45 people who do nothing but build custom strings. BowTech uses 22 strands (11 each of two colors) of high quality BCY 452X material that is pre-treated with a synthetic wax. Every set is pre-stretched at 450 psi and held for five minutes before serving is applied.

The patented Mathews Zebra ZS Twist strings use counterclockwise (Z) and clockwise (S) twisted filaments bundled together to make a complete string. This balances the string to dramatically reduce peep rotation. Also, the two-color design makes it easier to separate the strands for peep installation. Mathews Tiger Twist strings are made from Spectra/Vectran blend materials and have virtually no creep.

Winner's Choice strings and cables are constructed with a unique process that pre-elongates the string fibers so your string and cables stay at the desired length for the entire useful life of the product.

Most bowstring problems are caused by a hunter's negligence. When hunting, carry your bow with the riser down so if you do slip, the first part of the bow to contact the ground is the riser. Also, when winching your bow up and down from a tree stand, connect the pull rope to the bow limb — not the string.

SIMPLE STRING MAINTENANCE IS CRITICAL. THAT GENERALLY CONSISTS OF NOTHING MORE THAN REGULARLY WAXING YOUR STRING WITH A GOOD WAX.

If you shoot with your fingers or use a release aid without a string loop, that means you must crimp a nock set onto the string's serving. Don't over-crimp! Also, "string slap" on your bow arm will rapidly wear out a string. Learn proper shooting form so you never have the string slapping your arm. Don't place your bottom wheel or cam directly on the ground. When you do, the string and wax pick up debris that eventually acts like sandpaper and causes unnecessary wear. Never install a peep sight or other string accessory under full tension. Instead, use a bow press to relax string tension for these chores. If you don't, minute fibers or individual strands will break or be damaged.

Simple string maintenance is critical. That generally consists of nothing more than regularly waxing your string with a good wax. This helps prevent fiber-to-fiber abrasion, keeps the bundle of strands together, maintains and extends the life of the string and prevents water absorption.

The bowstring might not be the most exciting part of your pet bow-and-arrow setup, but it certainly is one of the most important. Simply being cognizant of the string in the field and performing some basic maintenance will keep your string from letting you down when the chips are on the line. ■

chapter 29

IS A CROSSBOW IN YOUR FUTURE?

▶ ONLY A HUNTER LIVING ON MARS the past five years could have missed the explosion of crossbow hunting in America. In fact, crossbow hunting is the fastest-growing segment of the deer hunting industry right now. The growth reminds me of how the popularity of muzzleloader hunting similarly exploded in the early 1990s with the introduction of the first in-line rifles.

The reasons for this growth are many. Perhaps most important is the fact that more states have legalized crossbow hunting during archery-only seasons. Tied to this uptick in regulation changes is the fact that many archers become crossbow hunters as they get older and find they can't draw a compound bow anymore. With more and more hunters reaching retirement age, that's a trend that will continue.

Crossbows are also easier to learn to shoot — and shoot accurately — at archery hunting distances than compound or recurve bows, making them an ideal way to introduce youngsters and spouses to bow hunting.

If you're part of the growing corps of bowhunters thinking about giving crossbow hunting a try, here are a few things to consider before you make a purchase.

ASSESSING THE OPTIONS

The first step in purchasing a crossbow should be a visit to a dealer to shoot several different models to see which one you like and shoot best. Crossbows are expensive. They are as much or more than a quality compound bow with accessories. Take your time handling and shooting as many different models as possible before making a final decision.

While there are still some crossbows sold with recurve limbs, the technology has advanced and most hunters choose a crossbows with cams and cable systems similar to those found on compound bows.

Make sure you try cocking the crossbow. There are two basic ways to do it. The most common is to use some sort of rope-cocking device. However, more crossbows are now being manufactured with a built-in crank cocking device. These bows cost a bit more money, but they are much easier to cock consistently, and you never have to worry about losing the cocking rope. Parker recently released a crossbow that cocks itself with a canister of compressed air.

As far as sighting devices go, hunters should choose some sort of scope. Most of these come in either zero or very low or variable magnification — 4X magnification would be the top-end power you'll ever need. There are many different reticle configurations, from a standard plex-type reticle to cross hairs with multiple horizontal stadia that can be dialed in for specific distances — much like bow sight pins can be set. Also popular are electronic red-dot scopes, which employ both single and multiple red dots. These are excellent choices, especially in low light conditions.

A quality crossbow will also have a reliable and easy-to-use safety, just like a rifle.

WHAT ABOUT ARROWS?

The shortened arrows a crossbow shoots (sometimes called "bolts") are being made by several top-end arrow makers. They have the same plastic fletches used by most compound bow shooters, and

employ the same screw-in arrow point system.

Some companies have begun selling beefy heads designed specifically for crossbow hunting. They are worth checking out. However, regardless of what weight (or design) you select, make sure you test your arrow/ broadhead combination on the range for accuracy and consistency. Then, sight the crossbow in using this identical combination before heading afield.

Many archers become crossbow hunters as they get older and find they can't draw a compound bow anymore. With more and more hunters reaching retirement age, that's a trend that will continue.

Because crossbows launch their arrows at faster initial speeds than most compounds, mechanical broadheads are very popular with many crossbow hunters. Just how fast will crossbows shoot? It is hard to find a quality hunting crossbow today that launches an arrow at less than 300 feet-per-second. Many surpass the 350 fps mark and some exceed 400 fps.

Because of these speeds — and the crossbow design — it is very important that you regularly lubricate the rails to reduce friction as the string sizzles across the metal rails and to help impede string wear. Testing has shown that not lubricating the rails after as little as five shots will significantly reduce raw arrow speed. You should also regularly wax your string and cable system, just as you do on your compound bow.

OTHER NECESSITIES

There are a couple of accessories worth considering. One is a sling. Crossbows can be heavy if you're traveling far to get to your stand. A sling helps a lot.

Another necessity is a top-quality broadhead target so you can practice diligently.

A third item to get is a laser rangefinder. Crossbows might be faster than compound bows, but their arrows still fly with a deeply-arcing trajectory. For that reason I never hit the woods without my Nikon Archer's Choice laser rangefinder.

Another good item to purchase is some sort of shooting stick or monopod that can attach to the crossbow itself and can be used both on the ground and when up in your tree stand. You'll find that crossbows are beefy, heavy and often a bit unwieldy. A rest helps immensely. That's why many crossbow hunters use tree stands that employ shooting rails on all sides.

HERE TO STAY

Despite continued grumbling from some compound and traditional bowhunters that crossbows are not bows, these tools are here to stay. Both vertical and horizontal bows have their pluses and minuses when it comes to hunting. To fair and open-minded deer hunters I say, why don't you check out crossbows and decide for yourself?

resources

Measuring Your Draw Length

Unlike a traditional recurve bow that can be drawn back to virtually any length, a compound bow will draw back only a specific distance before it stops (the wall).

Compound bows are designed to be shot from the full-draw position. If a compound bow is set for a 29-inch draw length, it should always be shot from the full 29-inch draw position. The bow cannot be over-drawn — to 30 or 31 inches, for example — without modifying the setup on the bow. The draw length on your bow must be set to match your size.

To measure your draw length, determine the length of your arm-span in inches. Stand with your arms out and palms facing forward. Don't stretch when measuring. Just stand naturally. Have someone help you, and measure from the tip of one middle finger to the other.

Then, simply divide that number by 2.5. The quotient is your proper draw length (in inches) for your body size.

Most compound bow owners set their bows for too much draw length, which results in poor shooting form, inaccuracy and a painful string slap on the forearm. You will better enjoy — and be more successful with — your new bow when it is fitted properly to your body. And if you are in doubt, go

Arm-Span ÷ 2.5 = Draw Length

with a little short draw length rather than a little longer.

Also, if you plan to shoot a string loop, generally subtract ½ inch of draw.

resources

Paper Tuning

Paper tuning is arguably the best method to finely tune a bow and arrow. It is also one of the most straightforward.

To paper tune your bow, stand about 4 to 6 feet from a sheet of paper held in a frame with a backstop behind the paper rack. Beforehand, it is important that you verify the correct arrow shaft is being used. Using an arrow shaft that is too stiff or too weak can prevent paper tuning from being fully effective.

It is wise to start with the nocking point set at 1/8-inch above center. It is also important that the arrow rest is properly set to ensure that the fletching does not make contact. Start with the center shot about 3/4- inch out from the riser to the center of the arrow shaft and the rest height set to be centered in the rest attachment hole in the riser. These are for right-handed shooters. Left-handed archers should use the reverse.

Tear Left: (Often indicates a weak spined arrow)

Tear left

1. Decrease the draw weight. Turn the limb bolts out equal turns. (No more than 5 full turns.)
2. Decrease the point weight. A lighter point will have some effect on increasing shaft stiffness. Too light of a point however, might cause unstable arrow flight.
3. If steps 1 and 2 don't reduce the length of the tear to your satisfaction, you might need to change to a stiffer shaft.
4. Some small tears can sometimes be improved by moving the arrow rest away from the riser. You may also need to add a twist or two to the yoke system on the opposite side of the tear. (For a left tear, add a couple twists to the right side of the yolk.)

Tear Right: (Often indicates an arrow that is too stiff)

1. Increase the draw weight. Tighten both limbs bolts in at equal turns.

Tear right

2. Increase point weight. A heavier point will have some effect on decreasing shaft stiffness. Arrow speed might be reduced.
3. If steps 1 and 2 don't reduce the length of the tear to your satisfaction, you might need to change to a shaft with less spine. Small tears can sometimes be improved by moving the arrow rest toward the riser. You may also need to add a twist or two to the yoke system on the opposite side of the tear. (For a left tear, add a couple twists to the right side of the yolk.)

To correct a high tear:

1. Move the nocking point down In small increments, or raise the rest height.
2. If using a launcher or shoot-through type arrow rest, move the arrow support arm up. Increasing spring tension can also be helpful.

High tear

3. Check for fletching interference, and adjust the rest position as needed.

To correct a low tear:

1. Move the nocking point up in small increments, or lower the rest height.
2. If using a launcher or shoot-through type arrow rest, move the arrow support arm down. Reduced spring tension can also be helpful for even finer adjustments.

Low tear

* If nothing changes, you can also see if you are getting nock pinch, or if using an aftermarket string, check the serving size, as it may be too thick.